SMALLTALK
with Style

Edward J. Klimas   Suzanne Skublics

David A. Thomas

An Alan R. Apt Book

PRENTICE HALL, UPPER SADDLE RIVER, NEW JERSEY 07458

Library of Congress Cataloging-in-Publication Data

Skubliks, Suzanne.
    Smalltalk with Style / Suzanne Skubliks, Edward Klimas, David
  Thomas : illustrations by Kathryn Finter.
        p.   cm.
    Includes bibliographical references and index.
    ISBN 0-13-165549-3
    1. Smalltalk (Computer program language) I. Klimas, Edward.
  II. Thomas, David, 1946-   . III. Title.
  QA76.73.S59S58   1996
  005.13'3--dc20   95-19278
                                                        CIP

Acquisitions editor: ALAN APT
Editorial/production supervision
  and interior design: SHARYN VITRANO
Cover designer: BRUCE KENSELAAR
Manufacturing buyer: DONNA SULLIVAN
Editorial assistant: SHIRLEY McGUIRE

Illustrations by Kathryn Finter and Doug Talbott

© 1996 by Prentice Hall, Inc.
A Simon & Schuster Company
Upper Saddle River, New Jersey 07458

The author and publisher of this book have used their best efforts in preparing this book. These efforts include the development, research, and testing of the theories and programs to determine their effectiveness. The author and publisher make no warranty of any kind, expressed or implied, with regard to these programs or the documentation contained in this book. The author and publisher shall not be liable in any event for incidental or consequential damages in connection with, or arising out of, the furnishing, performance, or use of these programs.

Printed in the United States of America

10 9 8 7 6 5 4 3 2

ISBN   0-13-165549-3

Prentice-Hall International (UK) Limited, London
Prentice-Hall of Australia Pty. Limited, Sydney
Prentice-Hall Canada Inc., Toronto
Prentice-Hall Hispanoamericana, S.A., Mexico
Prentice-Hall of India Private Limited, New Delhi
Prentice-Hall of Japan, Inc., Tokyo
Simon & Schuster Asia Pte. Ltd., Singapore
Editora Prentice-Hall do Brasil, Ltda., Rio de Janeiro

Dedication

This book was written for the general object-oriented and Smalltalk community to promote and further the overall development of object-oriented technology. The authors have donated all of the royalties from this book to support graduate students in the School of Computer Science at Carleton University.

CONTENTS

Contents

FOREWORD

When I was learning COBOL many years ago, I remember very well how much I benefited from reading a little book by Henry Ledgard and Louis Chmura entitled *Cobol with Style: Programming Proverbs*. They very succinctly captured the stylistic guidelines followed by experienced COBOL programmers. Good programming practices that might have taken me many months to discover were captured in a short manuscript that I could read and digest comfortably in a day or two. In this book, Suzanne Skublics, Ed Klimas, and Dave Thomas provide the same service to the growing Smalltalk community; ironically, a community increasingly populated by COBOL programmers moving to object technology.

Recently, I came across a group of inexperienced Smalltalk programmers who had been introduced to a technique known to Smalltalkers as lazy initialization. Lazy initialization is a time/space optimization that initializes state variables only if they are used. It is an appropriate technique to use when initializing a variable would take a long time or would use a significant amount of space. When, as practiced by this group, it is used for the initializing of all state variables it has a lot of disadvantages. This group and many others would have benefited greatly from reading the more than 100 guidelines contained in this book. This book communicates practices used by experienced Smalltalk programmers in a concise, unambiguous manner. The rationale for each guideline is explained, example uses given, and situations where following the guideline is and is not appropriate are described. This book will help you write Smalltalk code that is easy to read, easy to understand and, as a result, easier to reuse.

I am fortunate to have had the opportunity to work with all of the authors of this book in some capacity. I have learned much about Smalltalk from each of them. By reading this book, you will too. *Smalltalk with Style* is a valuable contribution to the Smalltalk literature and a "must read" for both beginning and experienced Smalltalk programmers.

John Pugh

PREFACE

"I've been trying for some time to develop a life style that doesn't require my presence."
Gary Trudeau

About Programming Style and Guidelines

Introduction

Programming remains an intensively collaborative process between groups of program readers and writers. Few programmers create programs which do not need to be read and understood in part or completely by others. At the same time, programming is a demanding and intensely private intellectual activity in which a programmer must concretely describe abstract concepts in a form sufficiently precise to be executed by a machine. This places a natural tension between program readers and program writers. Modern programming environments such as Smalltalk stress reuse through the availability of large volumes or source code and interface protocols. In a perfect world, all code would have highly readable documentation that is separate from the program. In practice, we must strike a balance between our responsibility as a reader and our responsibility as a writer.

The purpose of a programming style guide such as this book is to provide a basic vehicle for addressing the needs of readers and writers. In this book, we describe a minimal set of guidelines to facilitate the reading and writing of object-oriented code in Smalltalk. This book attempts to help bridge the gap between well-established software engineering principles and the actual practice of programming in an OOP language such as Smalltalk by presenting guidelines. The intention of the guidelines is to make source code clear, easy to read, and easy to understand. Such source code is more likely to be correct and reliable. It will be easier to adapt, maintain, and evolve.

Use and Abuse of Guidelines

This book is not the answer: it is a place to start. This book is not an introductory text about Smalltalk or a complete manual of the Smalltalk language. To learn Smalltalk, see the following texts by Goldberg and Robson [**Goldberg** 83], Smith [**Smith** 94], Budd [**Budd** 87], LaLonde [**LaLonde** 94A], LaLonde and Pugh [**LaLonde** 90], [**LaLonde** 94B], and Shafer, Herndon and Rozier [**Shafer** 93].

This book should be used as the first draft for your own guide to good Smalltalk style. The guidelines are a good starting point for code reviews. Many can be supported by automated tools. Some of the guidelines in this book are application specific and/or controversial. It is up to your software engineering process to refine and extend these guidelines to suit your project. Initially, any guideline is better than none.

Product management plays a key role in ensuring that the software produced during a project is efficient, correct, reliable, easily maintained, and easily ported. We recommend that management:

1. create a project-wide commitment to the production of high-quality code,

2. define project-specific coding standards and guidelines,

3. train project personnel in the contents and use of the standards and guidelines,

4. establish policies and procedures to check and enforce adherence, and

5. foster an understanding of why uniform adherence to the chosen coding standards is critical to product quality.

Consistent coding standards simplify the cost-effective provision of automated tools to support programmers and to check the quality of their product. They also provide a systematic basis for evaluating the quality of programming tools for acquisition or development.

Guidelines are **not** standards. They need to be used to reinforce communication between developers rather than to beat them over the head. The best guidelines are those that people want to follow because they appreciate the benefit. Blind enforcement of a matter that is of personal taste is not in the interest of the project as a whole.

Conventions

All examples of code are presented in the following monospaced font to distinguish it from normal text:

```
This is an example of how code appears.
```

Within source code, boldface is used to help distinguish different parts. These include messages in a code fragment and method names when defining a complete method. For example:

```
mostOf := adults size max: children size.
```

There are notes spread throughout the book. They can be considered as a side issue or a tidbit of information about Smalltalk. All of these asides are enclosed with a border.

> This is an example of an aside.

Boldface is used for emphasis, and when an important term is introduced for the first time or is defined in the glossary. For example:

When defining an **abstract class**, all details...

In the body of text, Smalltalk classes start with an upper case letter and are in italics, such as *String*. Method names are preceded by the # character, and are in boldface as in **#size**.

For each guideline, we provide examples to illustrate how to apply it. We also include examples that do not follow the guideline. Examples that follow the guideline are marked by the symbol ✔ while examples that do not are marked by the symbol ✘. An example that does not follow a guideline is not necessarily incorrect. It usually means that the example does not follow the conventions used in the Smalltalk community, or is inconsistent with other guidelines. Please note that many of the classes and methods used in the examples are not real classes in any dialect of Smalltalk. They are created to illustrate the guidelines. Any resemblance to real classes is coincidental.

Acknowledgments

We would like to acknowledge intellectual contributions from the following people: Brian Foote, Ralph Johnson, Bertrand Meyer, Roxanna Rochat, Brian Wilkerson, and Allen Wirfs-Brock as well as the following organizations: The Allen-Bradley Division of Rockwell International, Knowledge Systems Corporation, LINEA Engineering Inc., Object Technology International, Inc., and The Software Productivity Consortium. We wish to acknowledge Jim Christensen for the original draft of this book. The authors would also like to thank John Pugh for his early and constant support, and to Greg Adams, Sam Adams, Ken Auer, and S. Sridhar for their insightful feedback and numerous useful programming tips.

☕1

WHAT'S IN A NAME?

"A good name is better than riches."
 Miguel de Cervantes, Don Quixote

"I would rather make my name than inherit it."
 William Makepeace Thackeray

Introduction

Choosing a good name for an object, method, or variable is a problem common to all programming languages.[1] A good name is a subjective thing and will often depend on the project and the programming language. Through increased use of the language, conventions are established and informally agreed upon.

In this chapter, we present common naming conventions used in Smalltalk. These conventions are not cast in stone. However, other Smalltalk programmers will find it easier to read, understand, and reuse code if it follows guidelines such as these.

General Naming Guidelines

Choose names that clarify the object's purpose. Smalltalk allows identifiers to be of any length; all characters are significant. Long names are important but may be limited by the environments' screen real estate. Identifiers are the names used for variables, constants, methods, and components within a program.

Descriptive names require fewer explanatory comments. Unique pronunciation for names simplifies human communication and avoids confusion. These attributes are helpful in understanding programs.

☛ **Guideline 1**
Choose names that are descriptive.

Example
✔ `timeOfDay`
✘ `tod`

✔ `milliseconds`
✘ `millis`

✔ `editMenu`
✘ `eMenu`

☛ **Guideline 2**
Choose names that have a unique pronunciation.

---

[1] There is an excellent discussion of the impact of mnemonic names in [**Ledgard** 79] pp.121-126.

Example

"Does this mean that the size was just read (red) or is it the size to read (reed)?"

✘   readSize
✔   sizeToRead
✔   sizeJustRead

Upper and Lower Case Letters

The variable names used in a program can be more descriptive if compound words are used. However, there must be a visual way for readers to mentally separate words. Some programming languages use an underscore to separate the words. In Smalltalk, upper case letters are used. Upper case letters help the reader scan for particular identifiers. In Smalltalk, names are case sensitive: MaxLimit, maxLimit, maxlimit, and MAXLIMIT are all different.

Upper and lower case letters also distinguish variable scope. Variables beginning with an upper case letter (globals, classes, class variables, and pool dictionaries) are global to all methods within the definition scope of the variable. Method parameters, temporary variables, and instance variables begin with a lower case letter. By convention, class and instance method names begin with a lower case letter.

 Guideline 3

Begin class names, global variables, pool dictionaries, and class variables with an upper case letter. If a compound word is used, each word should begin with an upper case letter.

Example

Behavior	"class"
Display	"global variable"
CharacterConstants	"pool dictionary"
CurrentUser	"class variable in a class called User"

 Guideline 4

Begin instance variables, temporary variables, method parameters, and methods with a lower case letter. If a compound word is used, begin each word following the first word with an upper case letter.

Example

✔	address
✔	currentTime
✔	beforeNoon
✔	isLunchReady
✔	readyForNextItem
✗	readyfornextitem

> In a compound word, do not confuse a prefix or suffix with a word when trying to determine which words should begin with an upper case letter. For example, some readers may think that the "c" in #subclass should be upper case, but sub is a prefix, not a word. When in doubt about prefixes and suffixes, check a dictionary.

Class Names

Choose a class name that reveals the purpose of the class. Names should not be so generic that they are meaningless to a reader. On the other hand, names should not be so specific that they reduce modularity or limit code reuse. Choosing a general name for a class encourages its reuse. On the other hand, naming the class in the context of a specific project helps to assure that its use will be clear in that context. Both cases are needed.

☞ **Guideline 5**

Choose a name indicative of a classification of objects. Select the least restrictive name possible for a reusable class.

Example

✔	ProblemReport	
✗	Application	"too generic"
✔	TreeWalker	
✗	TreeWalkerForBinaryTrees	"too specific"

When choosing a class name, consider **name space collisions**. Prefixes can prevent collisions when other Smalltalk developers may accidentally use the same common class names for the same or a different purpose. For example, one project may have a class called *Node* which may conflict with a class called *Node* in another project. A solution to this problem is to name the new class *XYZNode* where XYZ is the name, prefix, or abbreviation of the project. Note however, that this discourages reuse; a generic *Node* class would perform the operations of both *Node* classes, if possible.

Guideline 6

To avoid name space collisions, add a prefix indicative of the project to the name of the class.

Example

✔ PRFormat   "PR abbreviation for ProblemReport"
✔ PublisherFormat   "...for an on-line publisher project"
✔ NASASpaceShip   "part of the NASA project"

When choosing a class name, the proper level of abstraction conveys information that is useful to a reader of an object-oriented program. The name should not imply anything about the implementation of the class. Using a physical name as opposed to a logical name may restrict future modifications of the class and limit its reuse. On the other hand, if you are implementing a class that is a specific data structure, you can make that obvious in the name.

Guideline 7

Avoid naming a class that implies anything about its implementation structure.

Example

"A database for Problem Reports that uses a Dictionary. There is no need to tell the user the implementation."

✔ PRDatabase
✘ PRDictionary

"A proper name that is stored as a String."

✔ ProperName
✘ ProperNameString

"This class is not implemented with a Set; it is a specialized Set."

✔ SortedSet

By adhering to conventions relating class names with parts of speech, programmers can *read* the code. **Natural language** makes the code more descriptive and encourages programmers to write programs that read well. If the class is modeling some concept in a domain with well-established naming conventions, use the conventions for the domain.

☞ **Guideline 8**

Create class names from words or phrases suggesting objects in natural language.

Example

✔ Terminal
✘ UserCommunicationsInterface

✔ RemoteControl
✘ RemControl

✔ RandomNumberGenerator
✘ NumGen

✔ Road
✘ AutomotiveTransportMedium

Variable Names: Semantic or Typed?

When choosing an appropriate name for a variable, the developer is faced with the decision: "Should I choose a name that conveys semantic meaning to tell the user how to use the variable, or should I choose a name that indicates the type of object the variable is storing?" There are good arguments for both styles. Let's review some of the rationale for each situation before presenting the guidelines in "State Variable Names" on page 8.

Semantic Variables

If a semantic name is chosen, the user of a class must make fewer assumptions about the code to know what type of object the variable returns. A semantic name is less restrictive than a type name. When modifying code, it is possible that a variable may change type but unless one redefines the method, the semantics of it will not change. We recommend that semantically meaningful names be used wherever possible.

Naming a variable **aString** seems to preclude the use of a class that conforms to String but is not necessarily a subclass of String. How does a designer indicate that instances of String and all of its subclasses are acceptable as values of the variable? This restriction is more significant in user-defined classes than system-base classes. The latter are better known to experienced programmers.

Example

In this example, the typed variable does not indicate how it will be used whereas the semantic variable does.

```
"Typed variable"
anInteger :=
    numberOfAdults size max: numberOfChildren size.

"Semantic variable"
newSizeOfArray :=
    numberOfAdults size max: numberOfChildren size.
```

The semantic naming convention is not always as obvious as in the above example. There are cases in which choosing a descriptive semantic name is difficult.

Typed Variables

Although the typed variable seems to help a user know what kind of object is stored, it can sometimes be too restrictive. In the following example, **aString** assumes that the element is an instance of the class *String*. This is useful information for a user but does not imply that any class supporting *String* protocols is also valid.

Example

If a typed name is chosen, the format typically used is:
```
a<Noun> such as aString or aCollection
an<Noun> such as anInteger or anOrderedCollection
names collect: [:aString | aString copyFrom: 1 to: 4]
```

A typed variable can be a problem. For example, if a developer knows that any type of object is valid, **anObject** is often the name chosen. The developer knows that a set of objects is valid but does not know an appropriate name for the set. For example, suppose a *String*, a *Symbol,* and nil are valid. A developer may be tempted to use the name **aStringOrSymbolOrNil**; however, most developers choose **aString** or **anObject**. **anObject** is a better choice with an accompanying comment that says, "anObject can be a String, a Symbol, or nil."

Mixing Typed and Semantic Variables

The current practice is to use a mixture of both semantic and typed variable names. Parameter names for a method are usually named after their type. Instance, class, and temporary variables usually use a semantic name. In some cases, a combination of both semantic and typed information is given in a name. Examples from the base classes include:

```
inject: initialValue into: aBinaryBlock
copyFrom: start to: stop
findFirst: aBlock ifNone: errorBlock
paddedTo: newLength with: anObject
ifTrue: trueBlock ifFalse: falseBlock
```

Semantically meaningful names should be used wherever possible. Comments should be used to describe the variable. In the example variable names **selectorToPerform** and **objectToBeForwarded**, the typed name describes the object as well. This is true in many of the base classes.

The following sections include the styles that are currently used for naming variables. Whichever style you choose, use it consistently.

State Variable Names

State variable names (instance variables, class variables, or class instance variables) are usually semantic based. A combination of semantic and type information is also used.

☛ **Guideline 9**
Form state variable names from words or phrases suggesting objects in natural language.

Example
"Class PhoneBook"
✔ phoneNumber
✘ number

✔ name
✘ labelForPerson

"Class VideoGame"
✔ player
✘ boardMan

✔ enemies
✘ badGuyList

✔ score
✘ value

Example

The class variable names in this example provide semantic information about the use of a constant.

"This has little meaning to a reader. No class variables are used. Constants are directly referenced."

✗
```
buttonEvent = 1
    ifTrue: [self doNothing].
buttonEvent = 0
    ifTrue: [self execute].
```

"Class variables have poor names, ButtonEvent1 and ButtonEvent0."

✗
```
buttonEvent = ButtonEvent1
    ifTrue: [self doNothing].
buttonEvent = ButtonEvent0
    ifTrue: [self execute].
```

"Class variables have good names, BeginMoveEvent and EndMoveEvent. #beginMoveEvent and #endMoveEvent are accessors for the class variables."

✔
```
buttonEvent = self class beginMoveEvent
        ifTrue: [self doNothing].
buttonEvent = self class endMoveEvent
        ifTrue: [self execute].
```

☞ **Guideline 10**

Use common nouns and phrases for objects that are not Boolean.

Example

"In class Face..."

✔ `nose`
✔ `expression`
✔ `numberOfFreckles`

"In class Vehicle..."

✔ `numberOfTires`
✔ `numberOfDoors`

"In class AlarmClock..."

✔ `time`
✔ `alarmTime`

"In class TypeSetter..."

✔ `page`
✔ `font`
✔ `outputDevice`

Guideline 11

Use predicate clauses or adjectives for Boolean objects or states. Do not use predicate clauses for non-Boolean states.

Example

"In class Face..."

✔ eyesOpen   "true if eyes are open"
✘ isHappy   "true if face shows a happy expression"
"isHappy implies a binary state limiting the use of this variable. Instead of storing whether or not the face is happy, the variable **expression,** from the example for Guideline 10 representing a tristate such as happy, sad and mellow, would be used in a method called **#isHappy** returning (expression = #happy)."

"In class Vehicle..."
✔ fourWheelDrive
✔ motorRunning

"In class AlarmClock..."
✔ alarmEnabled

Method Names

A method's purpose is easier to understand if its name is well chosen. A programmer is more inclined to reuse a method if its name suggests its behavior. When you are naming a method, choose a name such that someone reading the statement containing the method name can read the statement as if it were a sentence.

Guideline 12

Choose method names so that someone reading the statement containing the method can read the statement as if it were a sentence.

Example

✔ FileDescriptor seekTo: word from: self position
✘ FileDescriptor lseek: word whence: self position

Guideline 13

Use imperative verbs and phrases for methods which perform an action.[2]

Example

✔ Dog
    sit;
    lieDown;
    playDead.

✔ aReadStream peekWord
✘ aReadStream word

✔ aFace lookSurprised
✘ aFace surprised

✔ anAuctionBlock add: itemUpForSale
✔ File openOn: stream
✔ record deleteFieldAt: index

When interrogating an object for its class as in the method **#isString**, use the class name in the method name. This helps a user of the method know what the method is testing.

Guideline 14

Use a phrase beginning with a verb, such as *is* or *has*, for methods that answer a Boolean when interrogating the state of an object.

Example

"A method to test if an object is a String"
✔ isString

"A method to test if a Person is hungry"
✔ aPerson isHungry
✘ aPerson hungry

"A method to check if a Vehicle has four wheels"
✔ aVehicle hasFourWheels
✘ aVehicle fourWheels

---

[2] See [**Bentley** 86] for a detailed discussion of the little languages technique implied by this guideline.

☞ **Guideline 15**

Use common nouns for methods which answer a specific object.

Example

"Answer the next item on the auction block."

✔ `anAuctionBlock nextItem`

"This could be the current or the next item on the auction block."

✗ `anAuctionBlock item`

✔ `aFace expression`

☞ **Guideline 16**

Avoid the parameter type or name in the method name if you are using typed parameter names.

Example

✔ `fileSystem at: aKey put: aFile`
✗ `fileSystem atKey: aKey putFile: aFile`

"for semantic-based parameter names"
✔ `fileSystem atKey: index putFile: pathName`

"useful when your class has several #at:put: methods"
✔ `fileSystem definitionAt: aKey put: definition`

✔ `aFace changeTo: expression`
✗ `aFace changeExpressionTo: expression`

☞ **Guideline 17**

Use a verb with a preposition for methods that specify objects. Use the preposition **on:** when a method operates on another object.

Example

✔ `at: key put: anObject`
✔ `changeField: anInteger to: anObject`

✔ `ReadWriteStream on: aCollection.`
✗ `ReadWriteStream for: aCollection.`

✔ `File openOn: stream`
✗ `File with: stream`

✔ `display: anObject on: aMedium`
✗ `display: anObject using: aMedium`

What's in a Name?

Using **#new** to create new instances of an object is a common protocol throughout Smalltalk class libraries. However, the creation of an object may require information to initialize it. In this case, use more descriptive method names with parameters to create an object.

There are two general message styles for initializing instances. One style is to pass all of the required initialization information as parameters with the instance creation message send. This is done using a more descriptive method name than **#new:,** as this message is typically used to indicate the size of the new instance. The user is restricted to whatever public protocol the class defines. See "Public Versus Private Accessor Methods" on page 66 and the Glossary for the difference between public and private methods.

Another style is to have the user send **#new** to the class to create an instance. The user creating the instance must be aware of the instance variables that require initialization for expected behavior and set them up using the public-defined accessor methods. (See "Accessor Method Names" on page 15 for more information on public accessor methods) Any instance variables that must be initialized for an instance of a class to function properly should be set by the instance creation method **#new** and an **#initialize** instance method rather than relying on the user to set them.

☛ **Guideline 18**

Use **#new:** or **#new** only for instance creation methods. Use **#initialize** to set initial values for instance variables.

Example

The initialize method sets some or all instance variables to some default value. In either case, supplying public accessor methods gives the user the flexibility of changing the values.

```
new
    "Answer an initialized instance of the receiver."

    ^super new initialize.
```

```
new: anInteger
    "Answer an initialized instance of the receiver with the count set to
    anInteger."

    ^super new count: anInteger
```

In a situation where the initial value is crucial, do not rely on the user; **#new** or **#initialize** should initialize the values. For example, if aBeanCounter has a **total** instance variable, **total** should have an initial value of 0. If the class does not initialize it to 0, its default value is nil and the following message will fail:

```
BeanCounter new total + 1000.
```

☞ **Guideline 19**

If an object requires initialization by the user when created, use a descriptive method name that indicates the information required instead of defining **#new**. Derive the descriptive name from the instance variables that require initial values.

Example

The class method to create an instance of *BookEntry* must include the name and phone number supplied by the user.

```
BookEntry
    name: 'John'
    phoneNumber: '5551212'.
```

If the instance of *BookEntry* is created by **#new**, the object should be initialized by sending accessor methods. In this case, the *BookEntry* class relies on the user to set the name and phone number.

```
BookEntry new
    name: 'John';
    phoneNumber: '5551212'.
```

Guideline 19 should be followed only when user-supplied initialized parameters are mandatory. If an instance created by sending the **#new** method with no initialization would cause an error, a common practice is to override the behavior of **#new** so that it fails. For example, the *BookEntry* class might have **#new** defined:

```
new
    "Answer an error to prevent the creation of instances of the
    receiver that are not initialized. Instances must be created using
    #name:phoneNumber:."

    self error: 'Use name:phoneNumber: instead of new.'
```

The **#name:phoneNumber:** method must, of course, be changed so that it does not send the **#new** message:

```
name: name phoneNumber: phoneNumber
    "Answer an instance of the receiver with name (a String) and
    phoneNumber (a String) initialized to name and phoneNumber,
    respectively."

    ^super new
        name: name;
        phoneNumber: phoneNumber;
        yourself.
```

What's in a Name?

Accessor Method Names

Accessor methods are used to retrieve and update the values of the state variables (instance variables, class variables, class instance variables) of a class. They are often referred to as get methods or getters and set methods or setters of a class, respectively. It is common to have the underlying data structures associated with state variables evolve during Smalltalk development. Although an object can access its state variables directly, one way to easily adapt to the changes in representation and the underlying data structures is to use accessor methods.

 Guideline 20

Methods which **get** a state variable should have the same name as the state variable.

Example

✔ books
> "Answer the instance variable books (conforms to Collection).
> books represents the collection of Book objects held by the
> receiver."

> ^books

✗ getBooks
> "Answer the instance variable books (conforms to Collection).
> books represents the collection of Book objects held by the
> receiver."

> ^books

If a method uses a get method to access a state variable within the class but wants to supply a different get method for the user, such as one that returns a copy of the state variable's value, define a public get method for the user and follow Guideline 20 for naming. The get method for the class' internal use should be private and named with **basic** as the prefix (Guideline 21).

 Guideline 21

When two **get** methods are needed for the same state variable, for example one returning the actual object stored and one returning a copy, prefix the one returning the actual object with the word **basic**.

Example

✔ "Public instance method"
books
> "Answer a copy of the instance variable books. books
> represents the collection of Book objects held by the receiver. A
> copy is answered to prevent objects other than the receiver
> from changing the collection."

```
^self basicBooks copy
```

✔ "Private instance method"
basicBooks
> "Private - Answer the instance variable books. books
> represents the collection of Book objects held by the receiver."

```
^books
```

Guideline 22

Methods which **set** a state variable should have the same name as the state
variable, followed by a colon.

Example

✔ books: aCollection
> "Set the instance variable books (conforms to Collection). books
> represents the collection of Book objects held by the receiver."

```
books := aCollection
```

✘ setBooks: aCollection
> "Set the instance variable books (conforms to Collection). books
> represents the collection of Book objects held by the receiver."

```
books := aCollection
```

State variables that represent Boolean conditions are often not accessed by the
conventional accessor methods. The method names contain the name of the variable
in a verb phrase that indicates the value being set to true or false. The name of the get
method that simply returns the value of the variable has the word **is** as a prefix.

Guideline 23

Use two verb phrase method names to access Boolean state variables in
addition to using the standard accessor methods. Use a third phrase to return
the value of the variable prefixing the phrase by the word **is**. If necessary, use
a fourth phrase to negate the current state of the variable prefixing the phrase
by the word **negate**.

What's in a Name?

Example
"Instance methods in the *Method* class."

✔ `isPrivate`
> "Answers true if the method is private.
> Answer false if the method is public."

> `^self privateStatus`

`makePrivate`
> "Set the privateStatus to be true if the receiver is private."

> `self privateStatus: true.`

`makePublic`
> "Set the privateStatus to be false if the receiver is public."

> `self privateStatus: false.`

`negatePrivateStatus`
> "Set the privateStatus to be false if it is currently true, and true if
> it is currently false."

> `self privateStatus: self privateStatus not`

"The following example does not imply two states but rather a range of
values. The user may construe this as returning a number value of the time
remaining in an example *Timer* class."

✘ `timeRemaining`
> "Set the timeRemaining to true if the time remaining in the
> receiver is > 5."

> `timeRemaining := true.`

`noTimeRemaining`
> "Set the timeRemaining to false if the time remaining in the
> receiver is <= 5."

> `timeRemaining := false.`

`isTimeRemaining`
> "Answer the timeRemaining, a Boolean set to true if the
> time remaining in the receiver is > 5."

> `^timeRemaining`

Accessor Method Names

17

> The prefix **is** in a method name is not restricted to answering a state variable that represents a Boolean. It is used to answer any expression that evaluates to a Boolean, for example, the method **#isMemberOf:** in Object:
>
> ```
> isMemberOf: aClass
>         "Answer a Boolean which is true if aClass is the class of
>         the receiver. Answer false otherwise."
>
>         ^self class == aClass
> ```

Method Parameter Names

Method parameter names are usually typed but can be semantically based as well. Selecting descriptive names for parameters simplifies debugging by providing more information about an object's interface.

Whether the parameter name used is semantic or typed, the comment should contain information to describe the parameter's type or semantics, respectively. See Guideline 42 on page 31 for information about method comments.

Example

In this example, the typed parameter indicates that an *Integer* is expected but does not indicate how it will be used. The semantic parameter does not indicate the type expected but it indicates its purpose. Both methods should contain a comment to specify the expected parameter type and how it will be used.

"Typed parameter"
```
new: anInteger
    "Answer a new instance of the receiver with a size specified by
    anInteger."
```

"Semantic parameter"
```
new: size
    "Answer a new instance of the receiver with a size specified by
    size (an Integer)."
```

A typed name may indicate to a user that there is a restriction on the parameter. In the following example, a user might assume that only an instance of *String* is a valid object for the parameter aString. Alternately, the designer may have meant that any object which conforms to *String* is acceptable. As well as adding a comment to clarify the situation, a better parameter might be a semantic-based one such as **name**. When a parameter must be a specific class, state that in the comment.

Example

✗   `removeRecordNamed: aString from: recordHolder`
    "Remove the record with name aString from the recordHolder."

✔   `removeRecordNamed: name from: recordHolder`
    "Remove the record specified by name (a String)
    from the recordHolder (conforms to Collection)."

The following example illustrates that neither the typed or semantic parameters offer enough information. In the typed example, the first parameter is too restrictive while the second is too vague. In the semantic example, both parameters are vague. In both cases, the method comment is essential to explain the parameters because the user may not be able to look at the source to determine the correct types.

Example

"Typed parameter"
`perform: aSymbol with: anObject`
    "Answer the result of sending the binary message named
    aSymbol with anObject as the argument."

"Semantic parameter"
`perform: selector with: argument`
    "Answer the result of sending the binary message named
    selector (a Symbol) with argument (any Object)."

☛   **Guideline 24**

If using typed parameter names, choose a name that corresponds to the most general class of object expected as the argument to the method.

Example

If a collection is part of the list of arguments, then name the parameter **aCollection**. If a specific type of collection is required, such as **anOrderedCollection**, use it. Here is a partial list of other possible names for common objects:

✔   `aPoint`
✔   `aRectangle`
✔   `anInteger`
✔   `aFile`
✗   `aKey`   "violates the guideline if there is no class named Key"

☞ **Guideline 25**

Combine semantic and type information for parameter names that are the same type.

Example

✔ Triangle top: topPoint left: leftPoint right: rightPoint

✔ aWindow initSize: initRectangle minSize: minRectangle

✔ Form
   foregroundColor: foregroundColor
   backgroundColor: backgroundColor

Cryptic names for the arguments, such as **at:** w **put:** d, can cause programmers many hours of frustration. Programmers debugging code like this must read the method comment or source code to find out what the objects **w** and **d** really are. If the method code is cryptic, debugging becomes difficult and tedious.

Method Temporary Variable Names

The convention for naming temporary variables is the same as that for instance and class variables. They are usually semantic based. Some designers use a temporary variable within a method for more than one purpose. It is confusing and should be avoided.

☞ **Guideline 26**

Do not use the same temporary variable name within a scope for more than one purpose.

Example

"The last statement will not unlock the original record."

✘ | aRecord |
   aRecord := self indexRecord.
   aRecord lock: 12.
   aRecord := aRecord at: 12.
   self update: (aRecord at: 1) with: self newData.
   aRecord unlock: 12.

✔ | nestedRecord aRecord |
   nestedRecord := self indexRecord.
   nestedRecord lock: 12.
   aRecord := nestedRecord at: 12.
   self update: (aRecord at: 1) with: self newData.
   nestedRecord unlock: 12.

Numbers

Consistent expression of numbers and the use of variable names for numbers makes code easier to read. If a number is used more than once, it should be assigned to a variable. It is easier to maintain code if there is only one place that a number is defined. The following guidelines aid in the recognition of numbers.

 Guideline 27

Represent numbers in a consistent fashion. Choose context-relevant variable names to represent numbers.

Example

"To perform calculations using pi..."

✔
```
pi := 3.14159.
area := pi * radius squared.
```

"To represent the number 1/3 as a constant..."

✔
```
textDisplayRatio := 1/3.
```

✘
```
textDisplayRatio := 1.0/3.0.
textDisplayRatio := 0.33333333333333.
```

If a rational fraction is represented in a base that is terminating rather than repeating, it contains increased accuracy upon conversion to the machine base. For example, 1/3 is more accurate than 0.3333333333.

 Guideline 28

Do not use hard-coded numbers in an expression.

Example

✘
"In this example, 2.54 is the conversion rate used to convert inches into centimeters."
```
length := originalLength * 2.54.
```

✔
```
centimetersPerInch := 2.54.
length := originalLength * centimetersPerInch.
```

✔
"Pi is a well-known magic number so it would be recognized in this example."
```
area := 3.14159 * radius squared.
```

"There is often a method to answer pi in class *Float* so it is better to use the following:"

✔   `area := Float pi * radius squared.`

There may be circumstances in which a number can be more descriptive than a variable. These are context specific and occur with universally familiar concepts. For example, in the equation to convert Celsius to Fahrenheit, using numbers instead of variable names is acceptable:

`fahrenheit := 32 + (9/5 * celsius)`

Abbreviations

Abbreviations can save the programmer typing time but can often make it difficult for another programmer to read or maintain the code. It is best to spell out identifiers completely wherever practical. Moderation is in order, however. Long variable names can obscure the structure of the program. An abbreviation can be justified if it saves many characters over the full word only when it does not affect comprehension. Many abbreviations are ambiguous or unintelligible when used out of context. Where necessary, use universally recognized acronyms instead of abbreviations.

☞ **Guideline 29**
Spell out identifiers completely.

Example
✔   `receivedTime`
✘   `rcvdTime`
✘   `rTime`

✔   `animationState`
✘   `animSt`

☞ **Guideline 30**
When you need to abbreviate, use a consistent abbreviation strategy.

Example
✔   `Display`
`    setUpLeft: leftDisplayRect`
`    top: topDisplayRect`
`    bottom: bottomDisplayRect`
✘   `Display setUpLeft: rect top: topDispRect bottom: botRect`

The example for Guideline 30 illustrates a typical situation. The message **#setUpLeft:top:bottom:** does not fit on one line in this book with the variable names that were chosen; the line wraps. Following Guideline 60 on page 44, the keyword message was split onto separate lines. If shorter variable names had been chosen, the message might have fit on one line, as in the ✗ part of the example. A good descriptive name for a variable should not be sacrificed just to make a message fit on one line.

☛ **Guideline 31**

Use a short full name or a well-accepted acronym instead of an abbreviation.

Example

These are commonly accepted and widely used acronyms.

✔ `EDT for Eastern Daylight Time`
✔ `GMT for Greenwich Mean Time`
✔ `FFT for Fast Fourier Transform`

✔ `millisecondsToRun:`
✗ `mToRun:`   "m could be milliseconds, microseconds, or minutes"

☛ **Guideline 32**

Use the context of a project to shorten names, but avoid obscure jargon.

Example

Mathematical formulae often use single-letter names for variables. Continue this convention for mathematical equations where it would help the reader recall the formula:

A quadratic equation:
`(a * x + b) * x + c`

The roots of a quadratic equation:
`(b negated + (b squared - (4 * a * c)) sqrt) / (2 * a)`
`(b negated - (b squared - (4 * a * c)) sqrt) / (2 * a)`

In a **BinaryTree** project, using **left** instead of **leftBranch** is enough to convey the full meaning given the context.

In a **MemoryManagement** project, **gc** can be the abbreviation for garbage collection.

☞ **Guideline 33**

Avoid uncommon or ambiguous abbreviations out of context.

Example

Although **temp** is a common abbreviation, it could mean either temporary or temperature depending on the context.

Although gc is a common abbreviation in Smalltalk for garbage collection, it could mean graphical context in a windowing project. The abbreviation should be avoided unless the context is clear.

☞ **Guideline 34**

Maintain a list of accepted abbreviations for a project and use only those in the list.

2

COMMENTS

"I wish he would explain his explanation."
  Lord Byron

"Let thy words be few."
  ECCLESIASTES 5:2

Introduction

The purpose of this chapter is to discuss program comments for Smalltalk code. Design documents are not discussed.

Comments are an important part of a program. They help readers understand the code. We describe two kinds of comments: those describing code statements or fragments, and those that describe the overall behavior of a component. For the purposes of this chapter, we assume **basic Smalltalk** and that the comments are stored either in an external file or with the component.

Misspelled, ambiguous, misleading, incomplete, scattered, or grammatically incorrect comments do not help readers. Short and accurate passages are best since readers tend to skip long passages. Programmers should maintain comments with as much care as code. **An incorrect comment is often as misleading as no comment at all**. Well-written comments make it easier to read, understand, and use code. Guideline 68 on page 51 also applies to comments.

 Guideline 35
Make comments succinct, concise, and grammatically correct.

When deciding the level of detail of the comments, recall our adapted version of Goldilocks and the Three Bears:

1. Too many comments can clutter the code.

2. Too few comments can leave a reader confused.

3. Just the right number of comments should help a reader understand your code, help a developer reuse your code, and help a maintenance programmer maintain your code.

A good guideline to keep in mind when writing a comment is to assume that, at some future date, you will have to reuse or maintain the code. Add the comments that you believe will help you do this job.

The guidelines in this chapter suggest one possible scheme. It is up to you or your project team to determine the information to include in each comment level before a project starts. Whatever subset of guidelines you decide to follow, it is important to be consistent and accurate with your comments.

Comments

Code Comments

Comments placed within the source code of a method are intended for software maintainers. They should provide information which is difficult to extract from the program text. Use comments to emphasize the structure of code. Regardless of the particular style of comments, it is possible to include too much information. Having more comment lines than code lines does not imply that the code is easier to read.

☞ **Guideline 36**
Do not comment bad code - rewrite it.[3]

Component Comments

Comments for a component (application[4], class, and method) are intended for the user of the component to determine its purpose. These comments are crucial to a user who does not have source code. Component comments include specification, history, and implementation details. The specification includes the component's purpose, use, and subparts.

How these comments are organized and presented depends on the environment used. Store the comments with the component. If you are using basic Smalltalk, you have several options. For an application, store the comment in either a separate file or as the header of the file-in that contains the classes. For a class, you can either store the comment in a separate file or implement a class method called **#classComment** that answers the comment. For a method, store the comment with the source code at the beginning.

Applications

Application comments include an introduction and a history. They should be organized in a manner that provides a quick synopsis of the application's behavior followed by more details including revision history, a description of the source code, and machine and compiler dependencies.

---

[3] **[Kernighan** 78] pp.144.
[4] There is no official name for a Smalltalk component comprised of classes that together perform some useful function. A group of classes is often another level of reuse, part of a larger deliverable, or an entire deliverable. We use the term application. Applications, whether by that name or another, are supported by some dialects of Smalltalk as well as by some of the enhanced Smalltalk development environments. If the Smalltalk you are using supports the concept of an application, keep it in mind while reading this chapter. Otherwise, think of an application as a file-in comprised of related classes.

☞ **Guideline 37**

The comment for an application should typically include:

1. a short synopsis of what the application does
2. information describing important characteristics of the code
3. class definitions
4. copyright notices
5. author names, dates, and places
6. where to look for platform dependencies.

Example

Application: FaceDraw
> A stand-alone face drawing utility.

Description:
> This tool provides the user with a facility to draw faces on a window. The parts of a face are provided in a toolbar and can be copied and dragged about the window. The face and its parts can be grouped and treated as one object.

Classes defined: Face, Eye, Nose, Mouth, FaceWindow
Copyright: 1995 ABC Software Inc.
Author: J. Smith
Date: 4/22/95
Department: Silly Software Reuse
Dependencies: GenericSmalltalk 1.2, ABCMENUS R3.2

The information and the detail to which it is included in the component comment may depend on company policy. For example, a company's policy may require the copyright information at the class level or the method level. The information may also depend on the programming environment. In a team programming environment, for example, each method might be written by a different developer. The component comment could then include the name of the main contact for the component while each method would include the developer's name and date of change.

Classes

☞ **Guideline 38**

The comments of a Smalltalk class should typically include:

1. a short synopsis of its role in the system
2. information describing important characteristics of the code
3. collaborations
4. example usage
5. copyright notices
6. author names, dates, and department.

Example

Class: QuestionBox Class
    A dialog box which poses a question and solicits an answer from
    the user.
Description:
Collaborations: TextWidget, LabelWidget, DialogBox, Compiler
Example Usage:
    QuestionBox poseForEvaluation: 'Enter a value' default: '1'.
Copyright: 1995 ABC Software Inc.
Author: B.Jones
Date: 11/23/95
Department: Widget Manufacturing

Someone who is subclassing an abstract class needs to know which methods must be implemented for the subclass to function properly. The class comment should reflect this. See "Refactoring the Class Hierarchy – Abstract Classes" on page 67.

 Guideline 39

For an abstract class, the class comments should include methods that must be implemented by a subclass of the class.

Example

This example does not contain the complete class comment. It shows how to indicate that a class is abstract and how to indicate that the subclasses should implement some standard protocol.

Class: Widget
    The superclass of all standard widgets; an abstract class providing all of
    the common protocol for all of its subclasses. A Widget is a ...
Description:
    This class ...
Public Instance Protocol to be implemented by subclasses:
    #create
    #defaultAction
Copyright: 1994 ABC Software Inc.
Author: M. Moore
Date: 08/11/94
Department: Widget Manufacturing

Methods

Method comments should contain sufficient information for a user to know exactly how to use the method, what the method does including any side effects, and what it answers without having to look at the source code. The source code may not be available; thus, it cannot be relied upon to explain a method to a user. It is important to keep the comments synchronized with the implementation.

☞ **Guideline 40**

Maintain the method comments with as much care as the source code and keep them synchronized.

Use the active voice for method comments. It is stronger and easier to understand. The passive voice is weaker and can make a comment more difficult to write.

☞ **Guideline 41**

Use the active voice, not passive, when composing a method comment.

Example

✗ "Passive voice"

`createShell`

   "The receiver's shell is created. The focus callback is hooked."

✔ "Active voice"

`createShell`

   "Create the receiver's shell. Hook the focus callback."

If the method and parameters have descriptive names, the method comment can be more succinct. Restating the code is redundant. The comments in a method should contain information about the expected input, the use of the parameters, and the answered object. A cross reference to other methods that are used or related may also be useful to the user.

If the code uses a complex algorithm, it may assist readers to include a pseudo-code version of the algorithm in the comments or to reference text that describes the algorithm. Comments that describe the behavior of the method may be useful to a programmer interested in reusing it—for example, "O(n log n) time," "recursive," "may block due to entry calls," "accesses global variables," or a reference to "Topological sort, Knuth Volume I."

A lot of information is required to use a method. If the development environment supports separating a brief comment from a more detailed one, then include only the method synopsis with the method source code. The detailed information should be available if the user needs to see it.[5]

---

[5] Ideally, in a hypertext environment, a button labeled *more detail* would be displayed with the method comment.

Comments

Guideline 42

The comments of a Smalltalk method should typically include:

1. the method purpose (even if implemented or supplemented by a subclass)
2. the parameters and their types
3. the possible return values and their types
4. complex or tricky implementation details
5. example usage, if applicable, as a separate comment

Example

"Class Date class method"
nameOfMonth: index
    "Answer the month name, a Symbol from #January to #December,
    corresponding to the month index, an Integer from 1 to 12."

"Class QuestionBox class method"
pose: question **default:** answer
    "Open an instance of the receiver with question (an instance of String) as
    its question and answer (an instance of String) as its default answer. If
    the user selects OK, answer the user's response (an instance of String)
    after leading and trailing spaces are trimmed. If the user selects
    CANCEL, answer nil."

    "QuestionBox pose: 'Your name' default: String new"

Private methods[6] should have **Private** as the first word in the method comment. It is a convention in Smalltalk that if the word private is not included in the method comment, then the method is public; the word **Public** is not commonly used to denote public methods.

Guideline 43

Specify if a method is private by including the word **Private** as the first word in the method's comment.

Example

`fileld: aFileHandle`
    "Private - Set the receiver's file handle to aFileHandle."

Whether a state variable (instance, class, or class instance variable) is public or private, describe its purpose in the comment for the accessor methods. This comment is necessary for the user and the maintainer. If you include the descriptions of the

---

[6] See "Public Versus Private Messages" on page 60.

variables in an external document, the ideal situation is to automatically generate the
state variables section from the accessor method comments.

It is common to use **Answer** instead of **Return** in the get method comment.

☞   **Guideline 44**

Document the purpose of a state variable in its accessor methods.

Example

In the Date class for the instance variable day
day
    "Answer the number of days (an instance of Integer) from the
    receiver to January 1, 1901."

    ^day

Comments within Source Code

Good Smalltalk source code is self documenting, often making comments on
statements redundant. Statements need only be commented to draw the reader's
attention. If the source code implements an algorithm that requires explanation, then
the steps of the algorithm should be commented as needed.

☞   **Guideline 45**

Avoid relying on a comment to explain what could be reflected in the code.

Example

✗   "The comment replaces information that could be conveyed by the code."
     | i |
     i := 'Robin'.   "Assign the name Robin to i."

✗   "This code is obvious. The comment replicates information and is
     unnecessary."
     | name |
     name := 'Robin'.   "Assign the name Robin to name."

✔ | name |
     name := 'Robin'.

Comments

Guideline 46

When describing a set of statements, avoid restating the code.

Example

"This code fragment does not need a comment."

✔
```
| result |
result := self employees
    collect: [:employee | employee salary > amount].
```

✘
```
| result |
"Store the employees who have a salary greater than in result."
result := self employees
    collect: [:employee | employee salary > amount].
```

Guideline 47

Comment the steps of an algorithm, as needed.

From time to time, every programmer writes tricky code to cope with a performance problem, to work around a platform incompatibility, or to apply a temporary fix. It is essential to highlight these situations using comments. This signals the reader to look closer.

For example, highlight code that uses an assembly language user-defined primitive to perform some sort of synchronization. Call attention to this fact with comments. In addition to providing information about the assembly code, give an explanation for not using a higher-level Smalltalk construct. Explain why other methods did not work, such as "did not meet timing requirements" or "Smalltalk does not allow...". Leave the old code in the comment.

Another example is a comment explaining a workaround for a compiler bug. This type of comment is useful to maintenance programmers for historical purposes, and helps them avoid false starts.

Guideline 48

Use comments to highlight code that is non-portable, implementation-dependent, environment-dependent, or unusual.

Example

"Non-portable code example."
```
System showBusyCursorWhile: [    "Platform specific cursor"
    result := self employees
        collect: [:employee |
            employee salary > amount]].
^result
```

3

CODE FORMATTING

"Consistency is the last refuge of the unimaginative."
 Oscar Wilde

"You can be consistent or inconsistent, but don't be both."
 Albert Einstein

Introduction

This chapter includes guidelines that make source code easier to read. We define general principles of a good layout. We do not prescribe a particular formatting style. The decisions on the application of these principles is the responsibility of the project leader or organization.

In an environment such as Smalltalk, more time is spent reading code than writing it. The physical layout of source code on a page or screen can make it easier to read and understand. "A program is not only a set of instructions for a computer, but a set of instructions that must be understood by a human, especially the one who reads it the most - the programmer" [**Ledgard** 79]. It is more likely that others will reuse code if they can easily understand it. Proper formatting makes the maintenance of the code less prone to error by both the current developer and any future maintenance programmers.

Many of the formatting guidelines are based on the most common way people read and write Smalltalk code using a code browser. There is often a competing goal of trying to display as much useful information as possible while not making the user need to scroll. Given that screens vary in size and that some Smalltalk environments provide word wrapping, some of the guidelines may need to be adjusted.

One of the best ways of implementing formatting guidelines is to use a code formatter. An automatic coding template could include the guidelines. Since formatting styles are subjective, the ideal development environment would store the source code in some default format, and present the source code in whatever format the user prefers. Personal preferences may be different from the guidelines in this chapter. Those responsible for setting the conventions should recognize that an individual's satisfaction may be very important to a successful project. Each programmer believes that his or her style is the correct one. Be prepared to hear "That's not my style!" and relax the guidelines accordingly. For the sake of consistency, formatting could be deferred to automatic tools.

The most important guideline is consistency throughout the code and project. Ideally, everyone on the project should use the same style. If there are several programmers working on different classes within a project, then the same style should be used for every class. If a programmer chooses a particular style and another maintenance programmer modifies the class, the maintenance programmer should follow the style of the original programmer, regardless of philosophical agreement with the style. This keeps the style consistent.

☞ **Guideline 49**
Be consistent with your formatting style.

Method Template

☞ **Guideline 50**

Use the general template for a method:

```
message selector and argument names
    "A comment following the guidelines."

    | temporary variables |
    statements
```

The message selector and argument names begin at the left margin. If the method name and parameters are too long and do not fit on one line, follow Guideline 60 on page 44 for breaking up a selector onto more than one line. Indent all other lines by at least one tab stop. This allows the message selector to stand out.

A comment summarizing the message begins on the second line. See Guideline 42 on page 31 for what to include in the method comment. A blank line separates the comment from the temporary variable names, if any.

Example

```
includesKey: name
    "Answer true if the receiver has a key equal to name. Answer false
    otherwise. The parameter name must conform to Symbol."

    | index |
    index := self findKeyOrAnswerNilFor: name.
    ^self basicAt: index
```

Horizontal Spacing

These guidelines specify minimum spacing around messages and delimiters in various circumstances. The guidelines build on each other; follow and apply them in the order they are presented or they may appear to contradict each other.

Spacing makes the source code easier to read. Consistent spacing helps visual recognition of constructs, irrespective of where they occur in program text.

☞ **Guideline 51**

Employ a consistent spacing around messages and delimiters.

Binary operators are easier to distinguish when separated from other programming constructs such as variables. As a general guide, spaces are placed before and after binary operators; this is never incorrect. There are exceptions, however:

The **/** binary operator, when used with numbers, omits the surrounding spaces because of its use with fractions.

3/4 is more common than **3 / 4**.

However, use **numerator / denominator**.

The **,** binary operator for concatenation, by convention, omits the space before but not after because of its use as a punctuation mark in written language.

red, blue, yellow is more common than
red,blue,yellow or
red , blue , yellow.

☞ **Guideline 52**
Employ at least one blank before and after the following binary operators: *
+ < = > | := == <= >= and - used as a binary operator. Omit spaces on either side of the / binary operator. Precede the minus sign used as a unary operator by at least one blank.

Example

✔ `answer := (3 + 4 * 36) >= (32 + x).`
✘ `answer:=(3+4*36)>=(32+x).`

✔ `solution := (self > -20) | (self <= 100).`
✘ `solution := (self>-20)|(self<=100).`

✔ `aBlock := [:a :b | a > b].`
✘ `aBlock := [:a :b|a>b].`

"A block with temporary variables."
✔
```
aCollection collect: [:item |
    | string |
    string := item printString.
    Array with: string first with: string last].
```

✘
```
aCollection collect: [:item || string |
    string := item printString.
    Array with: string first with: string last]
```

The @ binary operator may have surrounding spaces depending on its arguments. This helps to distinguish the @ from a unary operator and from variables.

☛ **Guideline 53**

Omit spaces on either side of the @ message selector when both the receiver and the argument are positive integers. Otherwise, include the spaces.

Example

✔ 10@235
✘ 10 @ 235

✔ -10 @ -235
✘ -10@-235   "Omitting a space before the - is an error in some Smalltalks."

✔ 20 @ -15
✘ 20@-15

✔ xCoordinate @ yCoordinate
✘ xCoordinate@yCoordinate

The unary operator ^ (caret) for answering objects does not have a specific guideline for spacing. Most Smalltalkers do not leave a space between the ^ and the object being answered but it is acceptable to do so. Choose one way and use it throughout your code.

The guideline for parentheses is merely a convention and often seems to conflict with other guidelines. A more general rule to follow with parentheses is to make them easy to see and match up. This same guideline applies to brackets used as block delimiters.

☛ **Guideline 54**

Where parentheses ( ) delimit an expression or an argument list, leave at least one blank before the left parenthesis and after the right parenthesis but do not leave a space between multiple left or multiple right parentheses. It is not necessary to leave a blank after a left parenthesis or before a right parenthesis. This applies to block delimiters [ ] as well.

Example

✔ #((2 3) (3 4) (4 5))
✘ #((2 3)(3 4)(4 5))

✔ #((2 3))
✘ #((2 3))

✔ #(black white)
✘ #(black white)

✔ (4 + 5) * ((6 + 7)/(8 - 9))
✘ (4 + 5)*((6 + 7)/(8 - 9))

Spacing for the semicolon (;), colon (:), and comma (,) should follow the same rules as they do in written language: leave a space after but not before. This makes code more like sentences. The only exceptions are the colon (:) used to denote a block argument and the assignment operator (:=). In this case, no space is left between the two.

☛ **Guideline 55**

Leave at least one blank after but not before a comma (,), a semicolon (;), and a colon (:)when part of a selector. Do not leave a blank between a colon and an argument to a block.

Example

✔ `#(1 2 3), #(4 5 6).`
✘ `#(1 2 3),#(4 5 6).`

✔ `greeting := 'How are you Mr.', name, '?'.`
✘ `greeting:='How are you Mr.',name,'?'.`

✔ `result := 'lcm is:', (x lcm: y), '. gcm is:', (x gcm: y)`
✘ `result := 'lcm is:',(x lcm: y),'. gcm is:',(x gcm: y)`

✔
```
WidgetPen new
    black;
    home;
    turn: (90 + 45);
    turn: 90.
```

✘
```
"Violates Guideline 63 on page 48 as well."
WidgetPen new black;home;turn: (90 + 45); turn: 90.
```

✔ `value between: top and: bottom`
✘ `value between:top and:bottom`

✔
```
Array
    with: #(red blue green)
    with: 'Colors'.
```
✘
```
Array
    with:#(red blue green)
    with:'Colors'.
```

✔ `aBlock := [:x :y | x > y].`
✘ `aBlock := [: x : y | x > y].`

Leaving a space after a semicolon applies to cascading. If Guideline 63 on page 48 is always followed, then there is no need to be concerned with spacing after a semicolon – it will automatically be followed.

When a colon is part of a keyword message, there is no space before the colon because it is part of the selector. The space after the colon is to help distinguish the argument from the keyword.

Indentation and Alignment

Source code that is consistently indented is easier to read because the structure and flow of a program are easier to see. The reason for indentation is code clarity. Consistent indentation is more important than the actual number of spaces used. A modest level of indentation, such as one tab, is helpful to the reader.

Nested control structures and long expressions that span more than one line are easier to read if they are aligned on separate lines. Alignment can also reflect the flow of control of a program.

There is no absolute way to indent and align Smalltalk code. It is more important to be consistent within your code and, when changing someone else's code, to be consistent with their code. Be prepared to defend your style choices. Indentation and alignment seem to be the pet peeve of many Smalltalkers.

☛ **Guideline 56**
Indent and align nested control structures and continuation lines consistently.

Example
✗ "This example does not indent the **#at:put:** message consistently."
```
fieldName := (anArray at: 2) asSymbol.
fieldSize := (anArray at: 3) asNumber.
self fieldWidths at: fieldName put: fieldSize.
self fieldIndices
    at: fieldName
    put: anArray size.
```

✔
```
fieldName := (anArray at: 2) asSymbol.
fieldSize := (anArray at: 3) asNumber.
self fieldWidths at: fieldName put: fieldSize.
self fieldIndices at: fieldName put: anArray size.
```

✗ "This example has poor alignment making it difficult to read"
```
self phoneBook add:
    (Person new
    name: 'Robin';
    city: 'Ottawa';
    country: 'Canada').
```

✔
```
self phoneBook add:
    (Person new
        name: 'Robin';
        city: 'Ottawa';
        country: 'Canada').
```

If a statement is close to the right-hand margin, it would be acceptable to temporarily change this guideline on a local basis as long as the changes are consistent. This issue depends on the size of the screen, the width of the window used to view the code, and how important it is to avoid making the reader scroll.

 Guideline 57

Do not break a short expression across lines unless you have to, especially if it is a single keyword message.

Example

✔
```
self contracts remove: aContract ifAbsent: [^nil].
```

✔ "The style of this example is acceptable but it is not necessary to break this expression."
```
self contracts
    remove: aContract
    ifAbsent: [^nil].
```

✔
```
contracts isNil ifTrue: [contracts := Dictionary new].
```

✔ "The style of this example is acceptable but it is not necessary to break this expression."
```
contracts isNil
    ifTrue: [contracts := Dictionary new].
```

Guideline 58

Use indentation to delineate the logical nesting and match the alternative cases consistently when they exist.

Code Formatting

Example

"Blocks with short expressions contained on single lines."

✔ ```
^aPath last = separator
    ifTrue: [aPath]
    ifFalse: [aPath, (String with: separator)].
```

"Blocks with long expressions or more than one expression."

✔ ```
(word := scanner nextWord) first = $"
    ifTrue: [
        self addWord: word to: spec.
        inComment ifTrue: [^self].
        inComment := true]
    ifFalse: [
        word first isSeparator not
            ifTrue: [
                inComment not
                    ifTrue: [
                        self
                            addAllWords: spec to: body;
                            addWord: word to: body.
                        ^spec := OrderedCollection new]].
        self addWord: word to: spec].
```

✔ ```
(aDir := Directory
    opendir: aPath
    pattern: '*'
    mode: FREG) isError
        ifTrue: [^Array new].
```

---

 **Guideline 59**

To reflect control flow, indent blocks that follow iteration messages.

**Example**

✔ ```
contents
    do: [:each | tally := tally + each].
```

✔ ```
database
    select: [:dataEntry | dataEntry > 1024].
```

"...or..."

✔ ```
contents do: [:each | tally := tally + each].
```

✔ ```
self entries collect: [:entry | entry color].
```
```

✔   collectionOfPeople
         do: [:element |
             names add: (element at: 1).
             phones add: (element at: 2).
             postalCodes add: (element at: 3)].

     "...or..."

✔   [number <= 100] whileTrue: [
         sum := sum + number.
         number := number + 1].

✔   [number <= 100 and: [sum < upperLimit]]
         whileTrue: [
             sum := sum + number.
             number := number + 1].

✔   contents do: [:each |
         tally := tally + each.
         halves add: each / 2].

     "receiver expression is longer than one line."
✔   [self inputQueue isEmpty
      & self deviceQueue isEmpty
      & self deferredQueue isEmpty]
         whileFalse: [InputEvent waitForKeyboardActivity]

     "Although the *Blue Book* [**Goldberg** 83] uses this style, most programmers do
     not separate the opening bracket from the message."

✘   [number <= 100] whileTrue:
         [sum := sum + number.
             number := number + 1].

It is difficult to distinguish the keywords in a multi-keyword message that is long and,
as a result, wraps onto more than one line. It is easier to read the message if each
keyword is indented on a separate line from the receiver.

☛   **Guideline 60**
     Break up long keyword messages over multiple lines to avoid line wraps.
     Indent each line.

Example

"A multi-keyword message that has wrapped."

✗   (ClassPublisher new) outputFileName: 'exampleFile' source:
     MyClass printFormatter: SGMLFormatter
     includeInstanceMethods: true includeClassMethods: false
     generateIndex: true.

✔   (ClassPublisher new)
         outputFileName: 'exampleFile'
         source: MyClass
         printFormatter: SGMLFormatter
         includeInstanceMethods: true
         includeClassMethods: false
         generateIndex: true.

Sometimes, it is easier to read and understand a long keyword message in one line even
though it may force the user to scroll horizontally. In the example below, it is easier to
distinguish each menu item because each is on its own line.

```
Menu new
    addLabel: 'help' selector: #help enable: true;
    addLabel: 'edit' selector: #edit enable: true;
    addLabel: 'window' selector: #window enable: true;
    addLabel: 'file' selector: #file enable: false.

Menu new
    addLabel: 'help'
    selector: #help
    enable: true;

    addLabel: 'edit'
    selector: #edit
    enable: true;

    addLabel: 'window'
    selector: #window
    enable: true;

    addLabel: 'file'
    selector: #file
    enable: false.
```

There are many ways to align blocks and most developers have their favorite. It does not matter which style you choose, as long as you use it consistently. It makes your code easier to read and, with most styles, easier to visually check if you are missing any closing brackets.

☞ **Guideline 61**
Choose one way to align brackets in blocks and use it consistently.

Example
"The same example is used to show the difference in styles."

✔
```
selector first isLetter
    ifTrue: [
        (keyCount := selector occurrencesOf: $:) = 0
            ifTrue: [messageWordCount := 1]
            ifFalse: [messageWordCount := keyCount * 2]]
    ifFalse: [messageWordCount := 2].
```

✔
```
selector first isLetter
    ifTrue: [
        (keyCount := selector occurrencesOf: $:) = 0
            ifTrue: [
                messageWordCount := 1]
            ifFalse: [
                messageWordCount := keyCount * 2]]
    ifFalse: [
        messageWordCount := 2].
```

✔
```
selector first isLetter
    ifTrue: [
        (keyCount := selector occurrencesOf: $:) = 0
            ifTrue: [
                messageWordCount := 1
            ]
            ifFalse: [
                messageWordCount := keyCount * 2
            ]
    ]
    ifFalse: [
        messageWordCount := 2
    ].
```

Code Formatting

This section suggests a lot of rules that are specific to different kinds of messages such as multi-keyword, blocks as arguments, iteration, and alternative cases, and specific to the length of the source code line. A more general rule can be applied if it makes it easier. Some Smalltalk programmers always start a multi-keyword message on a separate line and put each keyword on its own line, whether the argument is a block or any other object. When a block is an argument, keep the opening bracket and the block arguments with the message and always start the expression on a new line, no matter how short or long it is. Applying this now to the specific examples used above:

```
someObject
    remove: anObject
    ifAbsent: [
        ^nil].

contracts isNil ifTrue: [contracts := Dictionary new].

selector first isLetter
    ifTrue: [
        (keyCount := selector occurrencesOf: $:) = 0
            ifTrue: [
                messageWordCount := 1]
            ifFalse: [
                messageWordCount := keyCount * 2]]
    ifFalse: [
        messageWordCount := 2].

contents do: [:each |
    tally := tally + each.
    halves add: each / 2].

[number <= 100 and: [sum < upperLimit]] whileTrue: [
    sum := sum + number.
    number := number + 1].
```

Cascaded Message Protocols

Using a cascaded message reduces the amount of typing required and reduces unnecessary clutter in the code. Cascaded messages are easier to follow when indented separately from the receiver.

 Guideline 62
Use a cascaded message instead of repeating the receiver object, including the case when the receiver object is **self**.

Example

✔
```
self
    label: self model label;
    minimumSize: 35@7;
    when: #reactivate perform: #reactivateWindow:;
    yourself.
```

✘
```
self label: self model label.
self minimumSize: 35@7.
self when: #reactivate perform: #reactivateWindow:.
```

☞ **Guideline 63**

In a cascaded message, separate the receiver object from the messages, each indented on a separate line.

Example

✔
```
self
    label: self label;
    minimumSize: 35@7;
    when: #reactivate perform: #reactivateWindow:;
    yourself.
```

✘
```
self label: self label; minimumSize: 35@7;
    when: #reactivate perform: #reactivateWindow:;
    yourself.
```

✔
```
outputStream
    nextPutAll: 'Customer name:';
    space;
    nextPutAll: self customer name;
    cr;
    nextPutAll: 'city:';
    nextPutAll: self customer city;
    nextPut: $.
```

✘
```
outputStream
    nextPutAll: 'Customer name:'; space;
    nextPutAll: self customer name; cr.
```

✔
```
^GenericMenu new
    title: 'File';
    owner: self;
    appendItem: 'New...' selector: #menuNew;
    appendItem: 'Open...' selector: #menuOpen;
    appendItem: 'Close' selector: #menuClose.
```

Cascaded message sends in which the messages are long or are multi-keyword can be difficult to distinguish from each other. A common practice is to either leave a blank line between subsequent message sends or to further indent subsequent keywords after the first.

☞ **Guideline 64**

Separate cascaded long key word messages with a blank line or further indent subsequent keywords after the first if the message has multiple keywords.

Example

✔ anOrderedCollection
```
    replaceFrom: 2
    to: 3
    with: #(a b c d e f g)
    startingAt: 3;

    replaceFrom: 7
    to: 8
    with: #(a b c d e f g)
    startingAt: 5.
```

✔ (ClassPublisher new)
```
    outputFileName: 'exampleFile'
        source: MyClass
        printFormatter: SGMLFormatter
        includeInstanceMethods: true
        includeClassMethods: false
        generateIndex: true;
    publish.
```

Number of Statements per Line

It is easier to locate variable assignments aligned along the left margin. A single statement[7] on each line makes statements easier to distinguish. Similarly, the structure of a compound statement is clearer when its parts are on separate lines. If the statement is longer than the remaining space on the line, continue it on the next line or restructure the code so it cascades onto separate lines.

---

[7] A source code statement is an expression that ends with a period or a semicolon.

Guideline 65

Start each statement on a new line. Use no more than one simple statement per line.

Example

✔
```
compositionRectangle := compositionRect copy.
text := aText.
textStyle := aTextStyle.
firstIndent := textStyle firstIndent.
rule := DefaultRule.
mask := DefaultMask.
```

✘
```
compositionRectangle := compositionRect copy.
text := aText. textStyle := aTextStyle.
firstIndent := textStyle firstIndent.
rule := DefaultRule. mask := DefaultMask.
```

✔
```
Fred := Man new
    hair: #black;
    eyes: #brown.
Wilma := Woman new
    hair: #red;
    eyes: #brown.
```

✘
```
Fred := Man new hair: #black; eyes: #brown.
Wilma := Woman new hair: #red; eyes: #brown.
```

☛ **Guideline 66**

If a binary or Boolean expression will not fit on a single line, break it up into subexpressions with the subexpressions placed on separate indented lines. Align the operators vertically to make the operations more visible.

Example

✔
```
receiverExpression
    + subexpression1
    * subexpression2.
```

✔
```
^(constants at: 'Overlapped')
    | (constants at: 'Clipchildren')
    | (constants at: 'Caption')
    | (constants at: 'Sysmenu')
    | (constants at: 'Maximizebox')
```

Code Formatting

Blank Lines

Blank lines are used to separate program fragments that perform different tasks, making it easier to read and understand the different fragments. They are not as necessary in Smalltalk as in other languages because Smalltalk methods are typically smaller.

Needing blank lines to separate sections may point out a method that is doing too many operations and needs to be split. A weak argument against blank lines is screen space. As Smalltalk methods are most commonly viewed in a browser on a screen, it is beneficial to be able to view the entire method in a window without having to scroll up and down. Most Smalltalk methods are 6-8 lines long [**Barry** 89] and fit into one window but the occasional method is longer and may require scrolling. If a blank line in a long method happens to fall at the bottom of a window, it is easy for the reader to assume that the method ends at the break.

☞ **Guideline 67**
Use a blank line to separate sections of code in a long method.

Source Code Line Length

There are many references that suggest the maximum line length should be between 70 and 80 characters so that they fit on a printed page. For example, the pretty printing standard for Pascal states that "Each line shall be less than or equal to 72 characters"[8] or the program layout convention "...keeping all lines shorter than 72 characters...or 80 characters..." so that the program text would fit on an 8.5x11 inch page.[9] Since most Smalltalk source code is read on-line, screen size (not paper width) often determines line length.

Long lines have a psychological impact. "Long lines retard reading speed, thus line lengths of more than 60 characters...should be avoided."[10] The approach in Smalltalk is to limit your line length so that a reader will not have to scroll horizontally to see the end of the line. We combine these two ideas into a guideline.

☞ **Guideline 68**
Limit source code line length to 60 characters or the window width, whichever is less.

---

[8] [**Ledgard** 79] pp. 163.
[9] [**Ledgard** 87] pp. 109.
[10] [**Baecker** 90] pp. 133.

Parentheses

Use parentheses to make the order of evaluation clear and explicit. Using parentheses in expressions that do not necessarily need them often simplifies the reading of the expression. Avoid redundant parentheses.

☞ **Guideline 69**

Use extra parentheses to simplify the reading of a complicated expression. Use parentheses to make the order of evaluation clear and explicit.

Example

✔ `frame width: (newFrame width * 4)`

"...is equivalent to, but slightly more readable than..."

✘ `frame width: newFrame width * 4`

"Extraneous parentheses"
✔ `maxAllowed := size * 2.`
✘ `maxAllowed := (size * 2).`

✔ `fahrenheit := 32 + (9/5 asFloat * celsius)`
✘ `fahrenheit := (32 + ((9/5 asFloat) * celsius))`

✔ `location y + (extent y - ((extent y - font ascent) // 2))`
✘ "The extra parentheses are not only cumbersome but cause the expression to wrap onto the next line."
`(location y) + ((extent y) - (((extent y) - (font ascent)) // 2))`

4

CAN YOUR SOFTWARE BE REUSED?

"Plagiarize! Plagiarize,
Let no one else's work evade your eyes."
  Tom Lehrer (adapted)

"I use not only all the brains I have, but all I can borrow."
  Woodrow Wilson

Introduction

The guidelines in this chapter deal with writing and exploiting reusable code. The underlying assumption is that developers rarely build reusable classes in isolation. The guidelines focus on how to produce reusable classes as a by-product of developing software for specific applications.

Reusable classes should fulfill a number of criteria:

1. They should be of high quality. They must be correct, reliable, and robust. An error or weakness in a reusable class may have far-reaching consequences. It is important that programmers have high confidence in classes offered for reuse.

2. They should be readily usable. The requirements for documenting reusable classes are more stringent than those for classes specific to a particular application.

3. They should be straightforward to adapt. Frequently, an otherwise reusable class will not quite fit the needs of the current application. If the original developer of a class anticipates changes, these could be implemented as skeleton methods (the method name and comment with no source code). A carefully structured class is easier to maintain and can often accommodate unanticipated changes. One way to achieve an adaptable class is by making it general. Providing a complete set of functions that a class might need in any context allows the use of a subset of the functions in a particular context.

4. If possible, they should be portable across platforms and domains. They may be used in different programs for different application domains, and in different dialects of Smalltalk.

Many of the guidelines in this chapter refer to and emphasize other guidelines in this book. The same considerations that affect the code's quality, clarity, and ability to be maintained and ported also affect the code's ability to be reused.

Common Protocols

Classes that have a similar interface should implement a common set of operations and use common terminology for protocols.[11]

---

[11] See the Glossary for the definition of protocol used throughout the book.

Can Your Software be Reused?

Goldberg and Robson [**Goldberg** 83] describe a common terminology that can be used with the following guidelines. The overall objective of these guidelines is to help a programmer reduce the number of different names used and increase the number of common names shared by a set of classes.

Consistent Messages

If one class communicates with several other classes, its interface to each of them should be the same for similar operations. If the name of the operation changes to add more arguments, it makes sense to make the names similar so readers of the program will see the connection. A common terminology supports polymorphism and increases the potential for reuse.

☞ **Guideline 70**
Adhere to a common terminology for naming. Use consistent names for similar operations.

Example

✗ Classes Line and Circle define the following operations for printing their contents:
```
outputOnPrinter, print, printLine, printCircle,
printLineInHexadecimal, output, writeItOnPaper
```

introducing several potentially synonomous names into the name space. These should all be defined as

✔ ```
print
```
or
✔ ```
print: options
```

The message **#print** is being sent to Line and Circle so there is no need to define separate methods.

Messages to Start, Initialize, and End

There is a common protocol used in Smalltalk for starting a program, opening a window, ending a program, closing a window, and initializing an instance. The following guidelines illustrate this protocol.

By convention, a programmer should be able to find how to start a program by examining the implementors of **#execute, #run, #start, #startUp,** or selectors that include these words as part of a compound word. Typically, sending **#open** or **#openOn:** opens a window.

 Guideline 71

Include the word **#open** or **#openOn:** in a method that opens a window. Include the word **#execute**, **#run**, **#start**, or **#startUp** in a method that starts a program. Choose and use one word consistently.

When creating and initializing new instances, a common protocol for the **#new** class method is of the form:

```
new
     "Answer an initialized instance of the receiver."

     ^super new initialize
```

If a subclass of this class is sent the **#new** message, it inherits the initialization method of the superclass. If the class needs a different initialization method than its superclass, it should implement its own **#initialize** method.

 Guideline 72

Define an instance method called **#initialize** to initialize instances created with the **#new** creation method.

Example
"An instance method to initialize the instance created. In this case, additional initialization is needed."
```
initialize
     "Use the superclass' initialize code and then initialize the
      receiver's count to 0."

     super initialize.
     self count: 0.
```

If you implement a class that sends **#initialize** from the **#new** class method to create and initialize instances, you should check if the superclass implements these methods as well. If the superclass implements **#new**, then you should not override it. If you do, you may cause your **#initialize** to be called twice, as in the example that follows.

 Guideline 73

If you need to create and initialize an instance using the **#new** and **#initialize** methods, check if the superclass already implements the same methods. If it does, then do not override the **#new** method.

Example

"In this example, blindly adding the ComplexNode subclass of Node means that ComplexNode overrides the #new method implemented in Node. As a result, Node's #initialize method never executes when creating an instance of ComplexNode. ComplexNode's #initialize executes twice. ComplexNode should inherit the #new method."

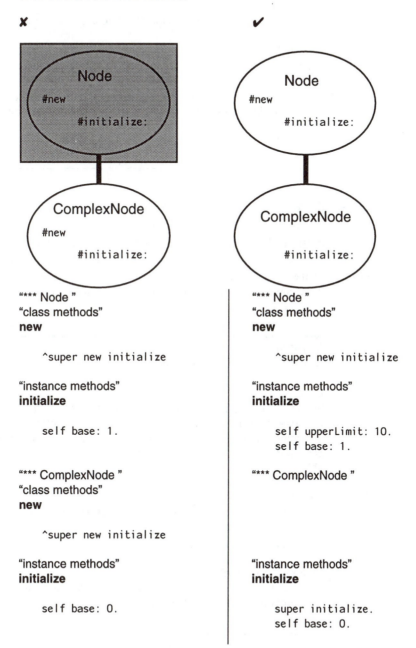

✗

"*** Node "
"class methods"
new

```
^super new initialize
```

"instance methods"
initialize

```
self base: 1.
```

"*** ComplexNode "
"class methods"
new

```
^super new initialize
```

"instance methods"
initialize

```
self base: 0.
```

✔

"*** Node "
"class methods"
new

```
^super new initialize
```

"instance methods"
initialize

```
self upperLimit: 10.
self base: 1.
```

"*** ComplexNode "

"instance methods"
initialize

```
super initialize.
self base: 0.
```

Related to **#open** is **#close** to close a window. If the **#close** method overrides that of the superclass, you may need to include a message send to the superclass' **#close**. Be careful of the placement of the message send to the superclass' **#close**; executing your code before the superclass' **#close** or after may have different results.

 Guideline 74

Check to see if a send to the superclass' **#close** is required.

Example

"Instance method to close the receiver. Additional behavior needed."
```
close
    "Clean up any extraneous file handles and then use the
    superclass' close method to close the receiver's window."

    self cleanUp.
    super close
```

Values Returned by Methods

The object returned by a method should be consistent with other related methods. For polymorphic messages, such as **#add:**, and messages with related behavior but different names, such as **#add:** and **#delete:**, the methods should answer the same object; for example, either the receiver or the parameter. Inconsistent return values can make a class more difficult to use.

 Guideline 75

Be consistent with the values answered from related methods.

Example

"In the incorrect part of this example, **#insert:** and **#remove:** are inconsistent because the former answers the receiver and the latter answers the parameter. In the two correct examples, **#insert:** and **#remove:** are consistent because they either both answer the receiver or both answer the object."

✗   `insert: anObject`
        "Insert anObject into the receiver. Answer the receiver."

        `self add: anObject`

✗   `remove: anObject`
        "Remove anObject from the receiver. Answer anObject if it is present. Otherwise, do nothing."

        `self remove: anObject ifAbsent: [].`
        `^anObject`

✔   `insert: anObject`
     "Insert anObject into the receiver. Answer the receiver."

     `self add: anObject.`

✔   `remove: anObject`
     "Remove anObject from the receiver. If anObject is not present,
     do nothing. Answer the receiver."

     `self remove: anObject ifAbsent: [].`

     "...or..."

✔   `insert: anObject`
     "Insert anObject into the receiver. Answer anObject."

     `self add: anObject.`
     `^anObject`

✔   `remove: anObject`
     "Remove anObject from the receiver. If anObject is not present,
     do nothing. Answer anObject."

     `self remove: anObject ifAbsent: [].`
     `^anObject`

> Do not assume that a method answers the receiver unless the interface description (method comment) explicitly says so.

Behavior of Well-Known Messages

Using polymorphism and common protocols throughout a system improves the potential for reuse. People assume that if a component has the same protocol, it will behave the same way.

If you are designing a class that implements a polymorphic message, be consistent with existing classes. If the class behaves as expected, it is more likely that it will be used correctly. Inconsistent method behavior increases the potential for error.

 Guideline 76
Avoid altering the behavior of well-known messages.

Example

Several classes implement the message

```
at: anIndex put: anObject
```

It is a common message with an assumed behavior. For example, the value answered from sending this message is always **anObject**. It would be inconsistent to implement a class with the **#at:put:** method that did not answer **anObject**. Inconsistent answers from the common protocols may result in difficulty using cascaded message protocols. If the class needs a message similar to **#at:put:** but cannot follow the common protocol, then give the message another name.

Several classes implement the message

```
add: anObject
```

It is a common message name. If the class you are implementing needs to perform some type of add operation, it would be beneficial to users of the class to use the same message name as long as the behavior is consistent with existing **#add:** messages.

Public Versus Private Messages

A public message will maintain consistent behavior and, if it does change in future development, the change will be well documented. A client can depend on a public method.

A private message is to be used by the implementor, not the client. Treat classes as a group developed by one person. A group contains one or more related classes, either related by a hierarchy, by collaborations, or both. Sending private messages is limited to within the group. No client class should send the private message.[12] Private messages exploit implementation knowledge of the representation and implementation of the class. They may change in future releases and cannot be relied upon.

☛ **Guideline 77**

Make a message private to indicate to other developers that its behavior is not guaranteed to remain consistent or compatible through future development. The private message may be sent within related classes developed by one developer.

---

[12]Enforcement of the public/private convention is implementation dependent. The notation that a method is private should be taken as a warning that although there is no restriction against using the method, the designer has not necessarily committed to keeping the method consistent in future revisions.

Limit Scope of Message Sends[13]

The Law of Demeter describes the message-sending structure of methods. Informally, the law says that each method can send messages to only a limited set of objects: to argument objects, to the **self** pseudo variable, and to the instance variables. The goal of the Law of Demeter is to reduce dependencies between classes. One class depends on another class when it sends messages defined in the other class. The Law of Demeter promotes maintainability and comprehensibility.[14]

"The style of modular programming encouraged by the Law of Demeter leads naturally to code that is easier to understand and maintain. The law lets you redesign classes (even their interfaces) while leaving more of the existing software intact. Furthermore, effectively reducing the effects of local changes to a software system can reduce many of the headaches of software maintenance. But following the law exacts a price. The greater the level of interface restriction, the greater the penalties are in terms of the number of methods, execution speed, number of arguments to methods, and sometimes code readability. In the long term, however, these prices are not fatal penalties."[15]

☞ **Guideline 78**
Implement a method such that it sends messages to a limited set of objects.

Example
"A chain of accessor message sends often indicates code that violates this guideline."

"Suppose we have classes called Book, Library, and ReferenceSection. Library has an instance variable called referenceSection. ReferenceSection has an instance variable called books."

✗ "Library instance method"
```
findBook: aBook
    "Answer true if the receiver contains aBook (Book).
    Answer false otherwise."

    ^self referenceSection books includesKey: aBook title.
```

"The Law of Demeter, thus the guideline, is violated because the object answered from the message **self referenceSection books** is not an instance variable in the Library receiver. This method relies on the implementation of books being a Dictionary, hence responding to the message **#includesKey:**. If you decided to change the implementation of books to be something other than a Dictionary, you would have to find all messages sent to books."

---

[13] The Law of Demeter discussed in this section is fully described in [**Lieberherr** 89].
[14] [**Lieberherr** 89] pp. 38.
[15] ibid, pp. 48.

✔   "Library instance method"
```
findBook: aBook
    "Answer true if the receiver contains aBook (Book).
    Answer false otherwise."

    ^self referenceSection includesBook: aBook.
```

"ReferenceSection instance method"
```
includesBook: aBook
    "Answer true if the receiver contains aBook (Book).
    Answer false otherwise."

    ^self books includesKey: aBook title.
```

Method Size

Smalltalk promotes the rapid development of reusable code. This depends on the fine granularity of methods: the smaller the method, the greater the probability that it can be reused. Well-designed Smalltalk methods are usually small.[16] It is easier to specialize a class with small methods. Although the occasional method may require many lines of code, this often indicates that a method is doing too much.[17] There is a strong correlation between a method's size and the number of defects. It is also easier to find errors in small segments of code. Consider breaking larger methods up into several smaller ones.

This is especially relevant when the class inheriting a method from a superclass needs most of the code in the inherited method, except for one part that needs to be slightly different. If the superclass has the behavior factored properly, the class can simply call the superclass' method and change the one or two lines needed.

    Guideline 79
Write small methods.

---

[16] An analysis of the Smalltalk image showed an average of 7.01 lines of code and 2.25 lines of comment per method [**Barry** 89].

[17] Exceptions to this guideline are often found in methods performing window layout code which, by their nature, can get very large, and in methods that interface to a monolithic component, such as an operating system.

         Can Your Software be Reused?

Misplaced Methods

It can sometimes be difficult to decide which class should implement a particular method. Messages with several arguments can sometimes be implemented as methods in the classes of any of its arguments. If a method does not send messages to the receiver or access its instance variables, then it should not be implemented in the class of the receiver.

☞ **Guideline 80**

Avoid implementing a method in a class in which it does not send messages to the receiver or access the receiver's instance variables.

Example

"This method does not access any instance variables and does not send any messages to self. It does not belong in this class."
"Class MailerConfiguration instance method."

```
formatComment: commentString defaultString: defaultString
    "Format a comment properly for being a parameter."

    | width maxWidth commentStream |
    commentStream := WriteStream on:
        (String new: commentString size).
    maxWidth := 65.
    commentStream nextPutAll: '    "'.
    width := 5.

    (String subStringsFor: commentString) do: [:substring |
        commentStream nextPutAll: substring.
        width := width + substring size + 1.
        width > maxWidth ifTrue: [
            width := 5.
            commentStream
                cr;
                nextPutAll: '    '].
        commentStream space].

commentStream
    cr;
    nextPutAll: '    DEFAULT: ';
    nextPutAll: defaultString;
    nextPut: $";
    cr.
^commentStream contents
```

Accessor Methods – Variable-Free Programming

In Smalltalk, state variables represent the state of an object. There are two ways to access the state from within a method:

1. Directly by name. Direct references to variables limit the ability of programmers to refine existing classes [Wirfs-Brock 89].

2. By sending an accessor message. The message is sent to self, which in turn accesses the variable by name and answers the value. This approach has significant benefits for reuse and maintenance.

Some programmers take issue with this guideline based on the perception that sending a message is less efficient than directly accessing a state variable. Compile time optimizations can eliminate overhead when using accessor methods [**Wirfs-Brock** 89].

Code that directly accesses state variables instead of using message sends may be shorter and easier to read but can be more difficult to subclass and reuse; the code is too dependent on the representation. It also makes it difficult to find every place where a variable is set. If you are stepping through a program and want to halt each time a particular variable is set, the easiest place to add a halt is in the set method. As a general rule, information hiding applies not just to hiding from others but from yourself as well: hide from yourself as much as possible [**Snyder** 86].[18]

 Guideline 81

For each instance variable defined by a class, define two accessor methods: one to retrieve the value of the variable (the get method), and one to set the value of the variable (the set method).

Example
"Instance methods in class Person."
name
> "Answer the name (String) of the receiver. name is used to uniquely identify the receiver."

> ^name

name: aString
> "Set the name (String) of the receiver. name is used to uniquely identify the receiver."

> name := aString

---

[18]There are excellent examples in [**Wirfs-Brock** 89] that demonstrate the variable-free programming guidelines.

Can Your Software be Reused?

☛ Guideline 82

Use accessor methods to reference state variables.

Example

"...assuming height and width are instance variables..."

✔ topRightCorner
"Answer the top right corner (Point) of the receiver."

```
^self height @ self width
```

✘ topRightCorner
"Answer the top right corner (Point) of the receiver."

```
^height @ width
```

☛ Guideline 83

An accessor method should do nothing but store or retrieve the value of its associated variable. Avoid computations that have no relevance to the variable being accessed.[19]

Example

This method does more than just set the instance variable **selectedReports**. It checks to see if only one report is selected and, if so, sets another instance variable, **selectedReport**, to store the single report.

✘ selectedReports: aCollection
"Set the selected reports."

```
| report |
selectedReports := aCollection.
report := selectedReports size = 1
    ifTrue: [self reportFor: selectedReports first].
self selectedReport: report
```

The developer did not need to make a special case if only one report was selected. The **selectedReport** instance variable was not needed. The other methods that use the **selectedReports** collection should take care of the case of a singleton report. In the application from which this code fragment was taken, the **selectedReports** was always handled as a collection so the special case of one report was automatically taken care of. This application had several gratuitous checks to see if **selectedReport** was nil.

✔ selectedReports: aCollection
"Set the selected reports."

```
selectedReports := aCollection
```

---

[19]This guideline can be relaxed when using lazy initialization or when the instance variable is no longer stored and must be computed.

Public Versus Private Accessor Methods

If you do not want another object to access a variable, you have two choices: either do not implement the accessor method, or make it private. The latter choice is recommended. See "Public Versus Private Messages" on page 60 for the implications of making a method private. If other objects need to access a variable, then the accessor methods for it should be public.

 Guideline 84
Only those state variables needed by other objects should have public accessor methods; otherwise, the methods should be private.

Class Evolution and Refactoring

> "The history of all hitherto existing society is the history of class struggles." Karl Marx 1848

Good classes, like good programs, need to be rewritten two or three times. One of the most important activities in improving the reuse of a group of classes is the reorganization of the classes and their methods. The reorganization activity is called *refactoring*. Refactoring removes duplicated code and migrates information to the most appropriate place in the class hierarchy. The observation that inheritance is not working or that code is difficult to understand and reuse is often a signal that it is time to consider refactoring the class hierarchy. One of the major activities in refactoring is the increased use of *abstract classes*. See [**Wirfs-Brock** 90] for more details on this subject.

Abstract Versus Concrete Classes

Abstract classes are class definitions whose sole purpose is to capture common behavior (protocols) for a family of concrete classes which are subclasses of the abstract classes. The concrete classes provide the class representation and method implementation or both. Abstract classes serve as descriptive roles; they are never instantiated.

 Guideline 85
Use abstract classes to refactor common code which operates on different representations.

Example
Consider an application which performs text processing:
ByteArray
  String
    Text

Can Your Software be Reused?

To internationalize the application for Asia-Pacific, a programmer uses "cut and paste reuse" to quickly implement a solution for double byte languages.
Array
        DBCSString
            DBCSText

Unfortunately, this leads to an unnecessary duplication of code and a potential loss of new features or bug fixes. For example, if someone defines a new search mechanism for Text, it will not automatically be replicated into the code for DBCSText. If someone fixes a bug in DBCSText, it will not appear in Text. The programmer copied the method because there was no way in the original class definition to change the representation of Text, which itself relied on String's representation.

One possible solution is to refactor the classes as follows:

String "an abstract class with all methods but no representation"
        Text "an abstract class with all methods applying to text"
            ByteText
            DBCSText

Refactoring the Class Hierarchy – Abstract Classes

When only a small amount of code is shared using inheritance, the class hierarchy may benefit from being refactored. In the example that follows, class *CheckingAccount* overrides the **#withdraw:** method that it inherits from class *SavingsAccount* because it does not allow this behavior. It might be better to move the methods in *SavingsAccount* that *CheckingAccount* inherits to *BankAccount*, a new superclass of *SavingsAccount*. *BankAccount* will probably be abstract. Class *CheckingAccount* can then become a subclass of *BankAccount*, and override the **#withdraw:** method to handle checks. *SavingsAccount* does not need to override any methods. Instance variables defined in *SavingsAccount* and used by *CheckingAccount* move to *BankAccount*.

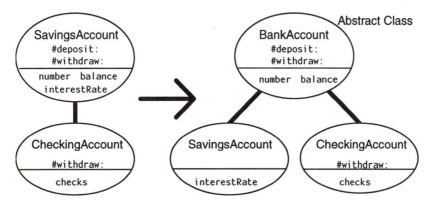

Abstract classes are usually refined out of groups of classes that share common behaviors. It is rare that the initial design and analysis phases of a project contain enough detail to identify many of the abstract classes. As the developer is implementing the classes, the abstract classes usually become apparent. They are used to avoid duplication of behavior, and to allow multiple representation.

Inheritance of Behavior Versus State

Many programmers familiar with data structure programming initially seize upon inheritance to share common aspects of representation. This is a common misuse of inheritance. Inheritance is used to organize families of classes which have similar behavior rather than similar representation.

 Guideline 86

Always inherit to obtain the behavior, not the representation.

Example

One possible representation for a process activation stack is a collection such as an array. However, just because an *Array* is a suitable representation does not make *Process* a suitable subclass of *Array*. In particular, *Array* defines a large number of operations which are not appropriate for a process. Furthermore, *Process* implements a number of operations, such as fork and suspend, which are clearly not array like.

✘   *Process* defined as a subclass of *Array*.

```
Array subclass: Process
    fork:   ...

    suspend:   ...
```

✔   *Process* should be implemented as a subclass of *Object* and use an array in its implementation.

```
Object subclass: Process
    instanceVariableNames: 'stack'

    fork:  ...

    suspend: ...
```

Can Your Software be Reused?

Subclasses Versus Subtypes

In an ideal world, all inheritance hierarchies would be subtype instead of subclass. A type is a specification of a behavior (specifies operations and their semantics), while a class is an implementation of that behavior.

A type S is a subtype of a type T if all objects of type S can be substituted for parameters of methods written to accept objects of type T. The benefits of subtype hierarchies are that every subtype can be used in any place where the type is used. This ability to substitute makes strict subtype hierarchies highly desirable. To guarantee a substitution relationship:

> S provides, at the least, the operations of T
>
> For each operation in T, the corresponding operation in S has the same number of parameters, and returns values consistently
>
> The types of parameters of operations in S are the same or supertypes of the corresponding parameters of operations in T (contravariance)
>
> The types of return values of operations in S are the same or subtypes of the results of corresponding operations in T (covariance)
>
> The specification of the external behavior is the same[**Thomson** 93].

In general, it is always desirable that class hierarchies be subtype hierarchies. However in practice, there are often cases such as singularities in representation and exception cases where strict subtyping is not possible. There are also cases where the choice of supertype is arbitrary, leading to confusing class hierarchies [**LaLonde** 91][**Snyder** 86].

 Guideline 87

Try to design subtypes instead of subclasses.

Parts Versus Inheritance: Part-of Versus Is-a

The browser and inheritance hierarchy is a convenient means for organizing descriptions of classes and groups of classes. It is not surprising, therefore, that novices often misuse inheritance to describe part hierarchies. Inheritance is used to organize families of classes with similar behavior. The part-of hierarchy is important for describing the relationship between a composite and its component parts.

 Guideline 88

Use inheritance to organize classes with similar behavior, not to describe composite objects which should be described using a part-of relationship.

Example

These are examples of parts, not inheritance:

House(rooms (walls, doors, windows), roof, foundation)

Car(body, engine(piston, camshaft), frame, wheels)

Tree (trunk, branch(leaf))

Unfortunately, the part-of relationship is not explicitly supported by most OO languages. Instance variables are used to hold the immediate constituent parts of each component of a composite but there is no linguistic support to describe the construction and structure of a composite. This is why design notations stress the need to identify and describe composites using the notation in one form or another.

Class Names and Pool Dictionaries

Many programmers are careful to avoid the use of global variables. However, they often liberally reference pool dictionary variables and class names. Following the theme of the Law Demeter, directly referencing a global variable or a class other than a base class requires additional dependence. This is especially true if the same global is referenced in more than one method within the class. What alternative is there? Just like state variables, the use of message passing greatly reduces the need to depend on the exact name of a variable. Using this approach, referencing a pool variable implicitly such as

```
stream nextPut: Lf    "Lf is a pool variable visible to the class."
```

changes to

```
stream nextPut: Character lf.[20]
```

> This example expression directly references a class but it is a base class.

 Guideline 89

Use message sending instead of directly referencing pool variables.

In the case of class names, developers often go through contortions trying to change classes which exist in the current image. They often give up and subclass them simply because they cannot make the system work while changing them. Window code for example, which could be isolated from the underlying window system, makes explicit reference to a particular implementation rather than doing it indirectly through a **constructor** class. See [**LaLonde** 89] for other uses of constructor classes.

---

[20]Various dialects of Smalltalk handle pool dictionary inheritance differently. This change eliminates these differences.

If you must send a message specifically to a global variable or another class, add a class variable to refer to the global or class and implement a method in your class that refers to the class variable. Use this method to indirectly access the global or class.

☞ **Guideline 90**

Avoid sending messages directly to global variables and classes other than base classes. If you must, then implement a class variable and a method to indirectly reference the global or class.

Example
Suppose that in a class you implemented, you need to access the default font of a *Font* class. Instead of sending the message **Font default** in a method that you implement, add a class variable called **fontClass** and add these methods:

"Class methods for ViewerClass"
```
fontClass
    "Answer the font class for the receiver."

    ^fontClass

fontClass: aClass
    "Set the font class for the receiver."

    fontClass := aClass

defaultFont
    "Answer the default font class for the receiver."

    ^self fontClass default

initialize
    "Set the default font class for the receiver."

    self fontClass: Font
```

Every method that needs the default font now sends the message **#defaultFont** to self. This code hides the fact that you are sending messages to a class and makes it easy to change the font class without having to change every reference to the class. For example, if you want to change the font class to *RemoteFont*, then simply send the message

```
ViewerClass fontClass: RemoteFont
```

5

Tips, Tricks, and Traps

"Experience is that marvelous thing that enables you to recognize a mistake when you make it again."
 F. P. Jones

"If I look confused, it's because I'm thinking."
 Sam Goldwyn

Introduction

This chapter offers tips and tricks about classic idioms and mistakes in Smalltalk and how to avoid them. Smalltalk, like other programming cultures, has its idioms and typical *first-time* mistakes. In time, Smalltalk programmers learn these idioms and how to live with them. They are not documented but rather learned by trial and error, and by talking to other Smalltalk programmers. While reading this chapter, experienced programmers may find themselves saying, "Oh yes, that one!" while the new programmer will hopefully appreciate the advance warning.[21] As with any other programming system, you may eventually compile your own list of favorites.

Common Syntactic Mistakes

Control Structures

In most programming languages, control structures have a distinct syntax. However, in Smalltalk, even the commonly used loop control structures are defined in terms of messages. The following are syntactically valid but semantically incorrect:

    [1 to: aCollection size] do: [....].

    (x < y) whileTrue: [....].

    [x isBig] ifTrue: [....].

Assumption of Return Values

Although the guidelines suggest that the return values of a method should be consistent within a class and across the Smalltalk library, there is no guideline to suggest what object should be answered. An unwritten guideline is to answer the object that makes the most sense. What makes sense to one designer may be nonsense to another. The object answered from a method may not be what you expect, thus should be checked and not assumed.

☞ **Guideline 91**
Do not assume that a method answers what you expect it to answer. Check the method comment or, if necessary, the code to verify the answered object.

---

[21] Some of these tips, tricks, and traps were compiled by Ralph Johnson in the USENET comp.lang.smalltalk forum in 1992. These tips were published in 1993 [**Johnson** 93].

Example

For every collection that grows, **#add:** answers the argument. Some people expect it to answer the receiver and get trapped with the following message send:

```
myCollection := OrderedCollection new
    add: #red;
    add: #blue;
    add: #green.
myCollection size.
```

The variable myCollection does not contain the new OrderedCollection. It contains the symbol #green. Sending **#size** to myCollection answers 5, not 3.

There are reasons why **#add:** answers the argument and not the receiver. It often means that fewer temporary variables are needed because the argument to **#add:** can be created on-the-fly and then other things can be done with the argument after the **#add:**. If you do not agree with this protocol, it is not a good idea to implement your own **#add:** that answers the receiver because you would confuse most other Smalltalk programmers who naturally assume a common well-behaved *add* protocol.

To avoid the specific problem of assigning the last argument added to a collection instead of the new collection, always send **#yourself** as the last message. The use of **#yourself** in the example that follows results in an OrderedCollection being placed in myCollection. Sending **#size** to myCollection now answers 3.

```
myCollection := OrderedCollection new
    add: #red;
    add: #blue;
    add: #green;
    yourself.
myCollection size.
```

 Guideline 92

When creating a collection using **#new** and the appropriate **#add:** protocol, send the message **#yourself** as the last message to the collection.

A classic mistake when beginning to program in Smalltalk, or when programming in a hurry, is to leave out the return statement in a method. Instead of the correct object being answered, the receiver is answered.

☞ **Guideline 93**

Explicitly return an object from a method if you do not want the receiver to be returned.

Example

The classic example of this user bug is to leave out the caret (^) in the **#new** method of a class. This is often referred to as the *caret-bug*. The **#new** method is supposed to answer an instance of the receiver and in this mistake, it answers the receiver, which is the class.

✗ new
    "Answer an initialized instance of the receiver."

```
    super new initialize
```

✔ new
    "Answer an initialized instance of the receiver."

```
    ^super new initialize
```

Should you explicitly return **self**? There is no rule for this. Either do it all the time or do not do it at all. Be consistent. Most developers do not explicitly return **self** when they want to answer the receiver because the dialects of Smalltalk can be relied upon to return **self** as the default. Regardless, the method comment should always state what is returned in, even if it is the receiver.

"Cut and Paste" Reuse

Reuse of code at the textual level by cutting and pasting is a common practice for rapid prototyping. Unfortunately, cutting and pasting of code subverts the reuse of modular code. It also creates significant unnecessary code bulk. Cutting and pasting code also creates problems because there is no automatic way to propagate change.

The term reuse is meant to refer to reusing code by sharing. If you are simply adding a pre- or post-condition to a method that you are inheriting, then do not copy the method source into your class. Send the message to super to perform the code.

 Guideline 94

Avoid cutting and pasting code if reuse is possible. If adding a pre- or post-condition, a message send to **super** should perform the bulk of the work.

Tips, Tricks, and Traps

Example

Class hierarchy for this example:

```
GenericPrompter
    TwoButtonPrompter
        TextPrompter
```

"Class GenericPrompter instance method"
```
initialize
    "Initialize the receiver."

    self
        done: false;
        result: nil
```

"Class TwoButtonPrompter instance method"
```
initialize
    "Initialize the receiver."

    super initialize.
    self
        button1Name: 'OK';
        button2Name: 'Cancel'
```

"Class TextPrompter instance method"
```
initialize
    "Initialize the receiver."

    super initialize.
    self
        messageString: '';
        result: ''
```

Common Yet Confusing Error Messages

Some syntax errors that occur when compiling a method do not always seem to report what you would expect. Although the experienced Smalltalk programmer is all too familiar with the following error messages, the new programmer is often initially confused by them.

☞ Guideline 95

An error message indicating **"does not understand self"** usually means that you have omitted the period at the end of a statement.[22]

Example

"Looking at this in the debugger will show **self** being sent to an instance of Float equal to 1.07."

```
| total subtotal taxRate |
subtotal := 1.
taxRate := 0.07.
total := subtotal * (1 + taxRate)
self printReceipt
```

☞ Guideline 96

An error message indicating **"does not understand whileTrue:"** usually means that the receiver of **#whileTrue:** is not a block.

Example

"The following line opens a debugger"

✘ `(number < limit) whileTrue: [do something]`

"The following line does not open a debugger"

✔ `[number < limit] whileTrue: [do something]`

When a "does not understand" error message occurs during runtime, check the spelling of the message and the syntax of the message send. It may be as simple as omitted parentheses.

☞ Guideline 97

Do not forget to use parentheses when sending several keyword messages in one expression.

Example

The error message **"between:and:ifTrue:ifFalse:" not understood** would result from the following code fragment:

✘
```
^myNumber between: low and: high
    ifTrue: [myNumber]
    ifFalse: [high].
```

"Parentheses are needed to separate the keyword messages."

✔
```
^(myNumber between: low and: high)
    ifTrue: [myNumber]
    ifFalse: [high].
```

---

[22]This message may vary in different dialects of Smalltalk.

Equality, Identity, and Equivalence

One source of potential confusion is the proper use of the = or ~= method to check for equality and the == or ~~ methods to check for identity. Class *Object* typically defines these two operations to be the same. Subclasses normally redefine the = or ~= equality methods as needed. When an equality method is overwritten, it is common practice to implement a **#hash** method. This method answers the same hash value for equal objects. Unequal objects may or may not answer the same hash value. The integer hash value that is answered is typically used by the Smalltalk system to index into a Dictionary [**LaLonde** 90A].

The == or ~~ identity operations should not be redefined by subclasses as they can change the fundamental behavior of the Smalltalk system. Two objects are identical if and only if their addresses in memory are the same: a == b iff address(a) = address(b). This condition may not hold if you override the identity operations.

Guideline 98
Do not override the identity == or ~~ operations.

Guideline 99
If equality = or ~= methods are implemented by subclasses, you should implement an associated **#hash** method to answer an integer value.

Example
```
Object subclass: #PostalLocation
    instanceVariableNames: 'city state postCode'
    classVariableNames: 'PostalLocations'
    poolDictionaries: ''
```

"Class PostalLocation instance methods"
```
= aPostalLocation
```
  "Answer true if the receiver is the same kind of object and has the same key as aPostalLocation. Answer false otherwise."

```
    ^self species == aPostalLocation species and:
        [self key = aPostalLocation key]
```

```
hash
```
  "Answer a hash value that is based upon the same information used to test equality."

```
    ^self key hash
```

```
key
```
  "Answer the information that uniquely identifies the receiver."

```
    ^postCode
```

Collections

It is not a safe practice to iterate over a collection that the iteration loop itself modifies. Elements of the collection may be moved during the iteration and, as a result, may be processed twice or missed. It is safer to make a copy of the collection and then iterate over the copy.

☛ **Guideline 100**
Avoid modifying a collection while iterating over it. Use the proper protocols or make a copy of the collection first.

Example

✗
```
aCollection do: [:element |
    element = someFilterCriteria
        ifTrue: [aCollection remove: element]].
```

At first glance, a developer might assume that the above enumeration will remove the desired element from the collection. Unfortunately, a closer examination of the statement's internal behavior will show that the position of the items in the collection changes after each element is removed and therefore the indexing into the collection is not correct during subsequent iterations. The following statements will perform the filtering properly:

✔
```
aCollection := aCollection reject: [:element |
    element = someFilterCriteria].
```

"or alternately..."

✔
```
aCollection copy do: [:element |
    element = someFilterCriteria
        ifTrue: [aCollection remove: element]].
```

It is a common practice for a class to implement an accessor method that answers a collection of objects that you can modify. However, some classes answer a copy of the collection to prevent you from modifying the original. Answering a copy indicates that you should not modify the original and should use the supplied interface methods to change the collection. This situation is often poorly documented.

The designer of an accessor method should either document this behavior to deter modification of the collection or, preferably, answer a copy of the collection.

☛ **Guideline 101**
Do not assume that an accessor method that answers a collection is answering the original collection; it may be answering a copy.

☞ **Guideline 102**

Answer a copy of a collection if you do not want the collection modified when accessed.

Another common error with collections relates to the Law of Demeter. See Guideline 78 on page 61 for more information. An example of how this guideline is applied to collections is shown in the following:

Example

✗ anObject tableOfThings remove: 12.

"This message relies on **#tableOfThings** answering a collection that understands **#remove:**. If the class does not provide the protocol to remove elements, such as a **#tableOfThingsRemove:** method, the code above is at risk of an error."

An extension of Guideline 78 applied to collections to avoid the example situation above can be followed. If a state variable is a collection, and either the class itself or another class needs to be able to add or remove elements from the collection, then implement accessor methods to perform this operation. The common naming convention for these accessor methods is the name of the state variable, in singular, with a prefix **add** and **remove** as required. If only **adding** is allowed, then do not implement the **remove** protocol.

☞ **Guideline 103**

Implement accessor methods to perform **add** and **remove** protocol for a state variable that is a collection.

Example

✔ "Class HotelRegistry with an instance variable called guests that is an *OrderedCollection*."

addGuest: aGuest
    "Add a guest to the collection of guests for the receiver."

    self guests add: aGuest.

removeGuest: aGuest
    "Remove a guest from the collection of guests for the receiver."

    self guests remove: aGuest ifAbsent: []

guests
    "Answer the collection (an instance of OrderedCollection)
    representing all of the guests in the receiver."

    ^guests

Creating Example Code

A common Smalltalk idiom is to include examples of usage as class methods. The example method's comment should include a line of code that can be executed from a browser by simply selecting the code and executing. The example should be in a separate comment. This allows the user to simply select the text between the double quotes and execute it. Some dialects of Smalltalk support *double click* to select everything within the double quotes.

Example
```
"class method in class MyClass"
example1
    "Calculate some value and answer the result."
    "MyClass example1"
```

Testing

Perhaps the most significant contribution to a commercial product's final quality is testing. Software requires the development of ancillary test code to verify the proper operation of the software and to verify that the software's operation is not inadvertently altered by modifications. This test code is often a significant percentage of the total product effort and, in some cases, more than the actual runtime functions [**Rettig** 91]. Unfortunately, in many organizations, the test suites are developed after the software is well developed, and often by groups that are not necessarily part of the original team. When testing is not done by the original team, the specific knowledge that the original code developers had of the system's intended operation is lost. When test suites are defined late in the development, the detection of defects is unnecessarily delayed. The longer the defect goes undetected, the higher the cost of fixing that defect.

Testing Smalltalk and object-oriented applications is an area of active research. To supplement this section, we suggest that the reader look at [**ACM** 94], [**Berard** 92], [**Beck** 94], [**Perry** 90], [**Rettig** 91], and [**Siepmann** 94] to get a more comprehensive view of testing.

Testing in Smalltalk

Testing in Smalltalk should be a seamless part of design and implementation. The normal practice is to exercise components as they are constructed rather than wait for a separate formal test. Classes are usually small and contain methods that only directly manipulate the data local to the object. Methods are quite small (typically 1-2 lines or 5-10 lines) and have a single function. Much of the work done by a class exploits predefined classes such as collections, thereby eliminating the need for any local data structures. The combined effect of modularity and the ability to exercise components as they are constructed eliminates the need for specific unit testing. It will take place naturally as a by-product of class development. Classes are developed and tested incrementally until several classes are combined into a component. These components can then be component tested.

One of the more attractive features of the Smalltalk environment is the support for building support tools such as test cases and test case managers. Test cases are just methods associated with each component. Test cases are written in Smalltalk and remain part of the product database. They form an integral part of the product and are often used as examples for demonstration. Class test cases exercise the basic functions provided by the class (a simple form of component testing). Use cases [**Jacobson** 92] exercise a set of components which satisfy a given requirement. Use cases describe application scenarios derived from requirements. Unlike class or component specific tests, use cases are designed to allow end-to-end testing based on real uses of the application under test.

At the unit and component level, design verification (in the form of code reviews) is the primary mechanism for ensuring the correctness of components. Component-level testing is used for functional verification and is usually provided with the design by the component developer so that it may be used in regression. This means that the number of test case methods per method is a small ratio (2:1 through 4:1, depending on the number of arguments in the protocol being tested). Consequently, the time spent writing test cases will not exceed the time to develop the software itself.

☞ **Guideline 104**
Test classes as they are developed.

☞ **Guideline 105**
Test components as they are integrated.

Reporting Test Results

The status of the tests can be displayed to the screen or to a window using standardized formats. Displaying the status to the screen or window may not always be desirable for several reasons:

> It may interfere with your testing if you are testing window code.

> It is not valuable if you are running a dialect of Smalltalk that allows you to run without a screen display.

> It may make your code non-portable between dialects of Smalltalk.

> It may slow down the testing procedure considerably.

We suggest that you implement a log device mechanism that can be specified as either the screen, a window, or a file for example. You then set the log device before you start testing. The results of testing can be logged to a file – or to several files, one for each class being tested – in a standard format. The log should contain a record of the successful and unsuccessful tests of classes and methods that have been performed.

☛ **Guideline 106**

Send error and log messages to a log device that can be specified.

Unit and Component Testing Approach

Unit Testing verifies that each line of new or modified code executes correctly. It exercises each new interface. Component Testing verifies that the new, modified, ported, and unchanged code functions correctly (as defined by the requirements). It exercises the external interfaces, functions, and data structures for a component. Component testing includes National Language Support (NLS) and help text testing as well as running code coverage tools to ensure 90% code coverage.

User Interface Testing

In practice, most graphical user interface (GUI) defects are not actually in the GUI. Seldom does the actual presentation component have defects, with the exception of operating system controls. The defects lie in the underlying application code or business logic, which in many first-generation GUI-based applications can only be exercised using the GUI.

By properly separating the GUI components (widgets) from the underlying application code and business logic (models), these components can be independently component tested using a conventional message-driven test case. This reduces the actual GUI testing to exercising the widget-model interconnection, which still requires either tedious human input or script files.

☛ **Guideline 107**

Interactive applications should be tested by exercising use cases.

Client-Server Testing

Assuming a reliable communication mechanism, client-server applications are actually straightforward to test. The client-server interface provides the actual test point. Both clients and servers should provide facilities to trace all messages sent between the two. In an environment in which communication is unreliable, it is essential to have some form of packet monitor to isolate communication problems.

Tips, Tricks, and Traps

Component Regression Testing

The objective of Component Regression Testing is to verify that the component still works after changes are made to the system. This test can detect unanticipated side effects and detect old defects that may have been masked. Key areas that should be executed during this test are:

> High-risk areas of the code; areas in which problems are often found.

> Areas of code that would cause the customer damage or down time if the code fails.

> Common usage areas; areas that the customer depends upon.

Do not assume that only a changed class and its subclasses need to be tested. There are many cases in which subclasses can affect data in their superclasses by using global variables or by accessing class variables. This situation is further complicated by the possibility that a subclass might inadvertently call superclass methods in an incorrect sequence and thereby create errors for other classes that need to interact with the superclass. For example, consider a subclass that erroneously instructs a superclass to clear a display window rather than put up a grid whenever a display command is received. Other subsequent operations might be expecting a grid to be on the screen.

There is no simple way to avoid complete testing of class hierarchies whenever a change is made. One might argue that testing superclasses is not required if the changes to the class do not access any superclass variables or superclass methods. However, it is impossible to automatically guarantee that such an interaction cannot occur [**Perry** 90]. There is a technique called **Extensions** [**Jacobson** 95] that facilitates software evolution while localizing testing to the portions of software that have actually changed.

 Guideline 108

All superclasses as well as subclasses of a class need to be tested whenever a change is made to the class.

A method that overrides another method can have different behavior from its superclass' method and needs to be tested accordingly. For example, a class may have a method to update a display window; there may be an optimized subclass that has the same overriding method which only updates the corrupted part of a display window. Both of these cases need separate test strategies to confirm proper behavior.

 Guideline 109

Every method in a class needs to be tested even if it overrides a superclass method and is tested in the superclass. Do not assume that a superclass' test method is adequate for testing a method that overrides it in a subclass.

System Testing

In this phase of testing, the primary emphasis is to use the product in a customer-like environment with concurrent product interaction. The focus is on a reliable, available, easy to install, and easy to service product with all the required functions within the environment. System Testing requires that all product use cases be executed.

Potential Sources of Abuse and Misuse

Every programming language has certain features that can be sources of trouble when misused. These features are included in the language to solve specific issues but can, if misapplied, result in code that is difficult to understand and maintain.

Global, Class, and Pool Variables

Smalltalk provides global variables, pool dictionaries, class variables, class instance variables, and instance variables for sharing information.

Global Variables

Global variables are directly accessible by all of the methods in a program. The problems with global variables in conventional software development have been well documented by William Wulf and Mary Shaw in [**Wulf** 73] during the "X considered harmful" wave of papers. The problems with globals in object-oriented programs were succinctly summarized by Bertrand Meyer in his article "Bidding Farewell to Globals" [**Meyer** 88] and are paraphrased as follows:

> As different modules share global variables, they make each of these modules more difficult to understand, read, and maintain.

> Global variables form a hidden dependency between modules. They are a major obstacle to software evolution because they make it harder to modify a module without having an impact on others.

> The use of global variables violates encapsulation and the protective software *fire walls* that result. It is much easier to make stand-alone portable applications and classes without global variables.

> They are a major source of errors. An error in one module may propagate to many others. As a result, the manifestation of the error may be remote from its cause, making it difficult to trace errors and correct them.

> Since a global variable does not belong to any one class in particular, it is not clear who is responsible for declaring and initializing the global.

Guideline 110

Avoid using global variables. Use class variables instead of global variables. If the value is to be shared by more than one class outside the class' hierarchy, then in the class containing the class variable, consider creating class methods that are the accessors for the class variable.

Example
The example on page 88 illustrates this guideline.

Class Variables

Class variables are visible to all instances of a class and its subclasses. A class variable is often a good replacement for a global variable. The class should include the protocol necessary to initialize the class variable, access it, and modify it as necessary. For example, suppose there is a class called *User* representing users of a system. Instead of using a global variable to store all the users, define a class variable called **Users**. The class protocol added to class *User* might include:

`#addUser:`	"add a User"
`#deleteUser:`	"delete a User"
`#deleteUser:ifAbsent:`	"delete a User, with absent block"
`#checkForUser:`	"check for inclusion"
`#users`	"answer the collection of users"

Guideline 111

Use class variables for shared components between all instances of a class and its subclasses.[23]

Pool Dictionaries

Pool dictionaries are the mechanism for sharing information between several classes. Pool dictionaries are usually used to hold related constants for a given application.

Guideline 112

Use pool dictionaries to group related symbols and symbolic constants that need to be shared between several classes.

Example
ColorConstants could be used to store all colors available in the system. This pool dictionary would map the color name to some constant representing the color.

---

[23]This guideline does not apply to class instance variables as they do not share their values with subclasses. Different values can be assigned to a superclass' class instance variables in each subclass. Class instance variables are not implemented in all dialects of Smalltalk.

In some Smalltalk circles, using pool variables is considered poor programming because they violate encapsulation.[24]

☞ **Guideline 113**

To avoid using pool dictionaries, use class variables with accessor methods. If the collection of objects stored in the class variable must be shared across several classes, create a separate class to hold the collection of objects in a class variable of the newly created class.[25]

☞ **Guideline 114**

To avoid creating hidden dependencies when replacing pool dictionaries with class variables, initialize class variables in a common initialization method.

Example

This example illustrates Guidelines 110, 113, and 114.
It is not a complete implementation. Only enough code is shown to illustrate the guidelines.

"Class *TextViewer* needs access to the values associated with various keystrokes, for example F1 to F9. The *TextViewer* performs some action depending on the keystroke. The keystrokes are also needed by several other classes (not shown). The constants are related so they are stored together in a class variable in a separate class instead of declaring **WindowControlKeys** as a pool dictionary or class variable in *TextViewer*. "

```
Object subclass: #WindowControlKeys
    instanceVariableNames: ''
    classVariableNames: 'ControlKeys '
    poolDictionaries: ''
```

```
"WindowControlKeys class methods"
controlKeys
```
"Answer the window control keys, a dictionary with the key as
the symbol representing a window control key and the value as
the operation to perform."

```
    ^ControlKeys.
```

```
controlKeys: aDictionary
```
"Set the value of the class variable."

```
    ControlKeys := aDictionary.
```

---

[24]Various dialects of Smalltalk handle pool dictionary inheritance differently. In some Smalltalk dialects, pool dictionaries are inherited by subclasses.

[25] See Guideline 90 on page 71 for an explanation of how to directly reference a class.

Tips, Tricks, and Traps

```
initialize
    "Set ControlKeys to a Dictionary and add the key constants."

    (self controlKeys: Dictionary new)
        at: #F9Key
        put: 120.

at: aSymbol
    "Answer the control key at aSymbol.
    Answer nil if aSymbol is absent."

    ^self controlKeys
        at: aSymbol
        ifAbsent: [nil].

at: aSymbol ifAbsent: aBlock
    "Answer the control key at aSymbol.
    Perform aBlock if aSymbol is absent."

    ^(self includes: aSymbol)
        ifTrue: [self controlKeys at: aSymbol]
        ifFalse: [aBlock value].

includes: aSymbol
    "Answer true if aSymbol is a control key.
    Answer false otherwise."

    ^self controlKeys includesKey: aSymbol.

Object subclass: #TextViewer
    instanceVariableNames: ''
    classVariableNames: ''
    poolDictionaries: ''

"TextViewer instance methods"

keyInput: anInteger
    "Process a key input (anInteger) to check if the window area
    should be cycled."

    anInteger = (WindowControlKeys at: #F9Key)
        ifTrue: [Notifier cycle].
```

Class Names Considered Harmful

If a method answers a new instance that is of the same class as the receiver, do not use the name of the class explicitly to create the new instance. To illustrate the potential problem, suppose *Array* contains the following method:

```
shrink
     "Answer a smaller copy of the receiver."

     ^Array new: self size // 100.
```

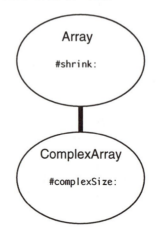

A new subclass of *Array* called *ComplexArray* defines the method **#complexSize**. Create an instance of *ComplexArray* and send the following messages:

```
| aComplexArray shrunkenArray |
aComplexArray := ComplexArray new: 300.
shrunkenArray := aComplexArray shrink.
shrunkenArray complexSize.   "causes runtime error"
```

ComplexArray understands the message **#complexSize** but *Array* does not. The code assumes that *ComplexArray* will inherit the **#shrink** method and will answer another instance of *ComplexArray*. However, **#shrink** explicitly uses the class name so it answers an *Array* instead. That means that **shrunkenArray** will not understand **#complexSize** because **shrunkenArray** will contain an instance of *Array* and not *ComplexArray* as intended.

This problem can be avoided by using **self class** to create a new instance in an instance method (use **self** in a class method) as shown in the following:

```
shrink
     "Answer a smaller copy of the receiver."

     ^self class new: self size // 100
```

☞   **Guideline 115**
Do not explicitly reference the class name to create new instances of the receiver.

Reduce the Use of Explicit Class Names

Class names are themselves global variables so reducing their appearance in the code improves reuse and makes the code more flexible.

 Guideline 116

Avoid using explicit class names.

Example

Consider an application which uses a set of Graphical User Interface (GUI) classes for various displays. It contains frequent explicit references to GUI classes throughout the code.

```
TextWindow new...
GraphicsWindow new...
TabularWindow new...
```

The classes references create an unnecessary dependency between the GUI and the application. Any change to the GUI will require a modification of the application. By introducing a class WindowSystem to encapsulate the GUI classes, the dependency is reduced.

```
WindowSystem text...
WindowSystem graphics...
WindowSystem tabular...
```

Gratuitous New Classes

Often, a novice will work on an application which uses a tiny variant of several classes such as adding simple pre- and post-processing code.

 Guideline 117

Unless a new abstraction is really needed, avoid defining a proliferation of new classes to accommodate minor variants that are seldom referenced.

Example

This new class overrides **#at:** and **#at:put:** to convert the key to lower case.

```
Dictionary subclass: #CaseInsensitiveDictionary
```

Using this in a single application does not justify introducing a new class since the application can handle this by changing the client uses of Dictionary to:

```
aDictionary at: key asLowercase
```

This is also an inappropriate way to specialize Dictionary since Dictionaries are not limited to keys that are strings. It is the key that needs specialization, not the container.

Use of become:

The Smalltalk message **#become:** is an expensive operation in some systems. It is a powerful and necessary operation for some special types of object mutations.

In general, **#become:** is used to change all references of one object to point to another object. The return value from **#become:** should not be relied upon. The behavior of **#become:** depends on the particular dialect of Smalltalk. Using the example,

    x become: y

The three behaviors are:

1. One-way **become:**
   All references to **x** now point to **y**; answer **y**

2. One-way **become:**
   All references to **x** now point to **y**; answer **x**

3. Two-way **become:**
   All references to **x** now point to **y**; all references to **y** now point to **x**; answer unspecified

An example using **#become:** can be found in [**LaLonde** 88], in which the authors include a case study that mutates unknown proxy objects into the proper objects.

 Guideline 118
Use **#become:** with caution.

Example
"FooClass public methods"

```
grow
    "Grow an array to a bigger array."

    | oldArray newArray |
    oldArray := self randomArray.
    newArray := oldArray class new: oldArray size * 2.
    1 to: oldArray size do: [:index |
        newArray at: index put: (oldArray at: index)].
    oldArray become: newArray

randomArray
    "Here is a random array"

    ^#(8 9 0)
```

Unwanted Instances

Sooner or later, a Smalltalk developer discovers unwanted instances of a class that are causing problems in the image. These unwanted instances can come from several sources, such as a failed window operation that may have had a runtime error, a global variable, or a sort block maintaining references to its last arguments. If you cannot find the unwanted instances, as a last resort you can use **#become:** to mutate them into empty Strings.

Example
The following code on some implementations of Smalltalk that support two-way **#become:** will not only mutate all pointers of the unwanted instances to nil but will also mutate all nil pointers to become instances of wanted objects and, more than likely, will cause a crash.

✘
```
ClassToChange allInstances do: [:i |
    i become: nil].
```

If you cannot find the unwanted instances, as a last resort, on dialects that support one-way **#become:** or two-way **#become:**, use the following code instead:

✔
```
ClassToChange allInstances do: [:i |
    i become: String new].
```

Unwanted instances are now automatically garbage collected. The objects that pointed to these instances now point to empty Strings.

Lazy Initialization

Lazy initialization is a time/space optimization that initializes state variables only if they are used. As illustrated in the example, lazy initialization is implemented by having the get accessor method perform the variable assignment when the variable is accessed the first time. It should only be used when initializing a variable would take too long or if a variable would use a significant amount of space that is not required most of the time.

As with optimization, lazy initialization should be used when appropriate. The following problems can occur if it is not used properly:

1. Haphazardly combining lazy and real initialization scatters the initialization code and makes initialization confusing.

2. During debugging, it is common to send the get accessor message for the variable to see the value rather than inspecting **self** to find the value. If the variable was still nil, sending the get message would initialize it.

3. You risk spreading out your initialization code, making it more complex for subclassing. Subclasses would have to either override the accessors to initialize the state to something else or preinitialize it, possibly using an initialization method (hence adding more confusion).

☞ **Guideline 119**

Use lazy initialization only when initializing a variable would take too long or if a variable would use a significant amount of space that is not required most of the time. Do not use lazy initialization in frequently sent messages.

Example

✔ `folders`
"Answer the collection of folders in the receiver's directory."

```
folders isNil
    ifTrue: [folders := OrderedCollection new].
^folders
```

✔ `foregroundColor`
"Answer the foreground color of the receiver window."

```
foregroundColor isNil
    ifTrue: [foregroundColor := Color black].
^foregroundColor
```

✘ "Each time **#asLowercase** is sent to a Character, **#isNil** and **#ifTrue:** are sent."

"class Character instance method."
`asLowercase`
"Answer the lowercase equivalent of the receiver."

```
LowercaseTable isNil
    ifTrue: [self initializeLowercaseTable].
^LowercaseTable at: self
```

Modifying the Base System Classes

"Don't perform brain surgery on yourself"

One of the significant benefits of Smalltalk is that most of the source code comes with the system. This permits the user to not only learn from the examples in the system, but to modify the system. The ability to modify the system needs to be tempered by an understanding that any changes made to the behavior of the system base classes can have significant repercussions. Modifications to the base classes affect not only a single application, but can have a drastic impact on a whole organization. Such changes can affect the expected and well-understood behavior which is relied upon by other internal developers as well as third-party packages that depend upon the base classes.

☞ **Guideline 120**
Avoid modifying the existing behavior of base system classes.

If you absolutely must modify the base classes, consider one of the following approaches:

Add an Application-Specific Method

If you need to make a small number of references to a single modified method, add the method using your own method. Give it a name that stands out, and make it private.

Example

```
Collection
    myAppAt: index put: value;
    myAppAt: anotherIndex put: anotherValue
```

Add an Application-Specific Subclass

If you need to change several methods, consider adding an application-specific subclass.

Example

Suppose you want to enhance the Inspector class so that you can ask for more information on the object being inspected.

✘   You modify the Inspector class so that you have a new option on one of the menus that allows you to, for example, browse the superclass of the object being inspected. The change you made has an error. All Inspectors are broken. When testing your code, you get a walkback and you try to inspect the objects in the debugger. It is broken as well because in breaking the Inspector, you also broke the inspector part of the Debugger. You can no longer debug your code and you must remove your changes just to use your image again.

✔   If instead of modifying the actual Inspector class you create a subclass called MyInspector, your error in the code would not have broken the system Inspector or Debugger and you would be able to debug your code and fix it. Once you are certain that your code works, you can modify the system mechanism to inspect objects to use MyInspector.

Case Analysis and Nested Conditions

Case analysis often results in code that is more difficult to maintain reliably. Subsequent developers must find every occurrence of the case statements in the system and make sure that all of them are properly updated. Case analysis also greatly reduces the ability to reuse the code.

Example
"This is not object-oriented code."

```
(anObject isMemberOf: Rectangle)
    ifTrue: [anObject drawRectangle].
(anObject isMemberOf: Circle)
    ifTrue: [anObject drawCircle].
(anObject isMemberOf: Line)
    ifTrue: [anObject drawLine].
```

One of major benefits of OOP is that the message dispatcher eliminates the need for most case analysis. Message dispatching and polymorphism provide a simple and efficient solution. With polymorphism, there are many objects that respond to the same command. Each object implements a common command such as **#draw** so that wherever an object needs to be drawn, one simply sends the following message:

```
anObject draw.
```

A **#draw** method needs to be defined only once for each object as follows.

```
"In the Rectangle class..."
draw
    "Code to draw a Rectangle"

"In the Circle class..."
draw
    "Code to draw a Circle"

"In the Line class..."
draw
    "Code to draw a Line"

etc...
```

Appropriate actions are taken by each object to implement its own drawing. The developer of a new object simply implements a **#draw** method for the new object; there is no case statement to modify or search for. In addition to simplified programming, polymorphic programming uses the message dispatching scheme for achieving the desired result, which is quicker than a case statement.

 Guideline 121
To simplify code, avoid case statements. Use message dispatching.

Checking for Class Membership

Checking an object for class membership is a thinly disguised case statement. Using code with multiple calls to **#isKindOf:**, **#isMemberOf:** or code of the form:

✗   "class Window instance method"

```
resizeToMaxScreen
    "Resize the receiver to the full screen size if it is not a
    FixedWindow. Do nothing if it is."

    (self class == FixedWindow)
        ifTrue: [self resizeNotAllowed]
        ifFalse: [self resize]
```

is often an indication of a function being in the wrong class. Replace these statements with a message to the object whose class is being checked. Create methods in the various classes of the object that respond to the message. Each method should contain one clause of the cases.

✔ "class Window instance method"
```
resizeToMaxScreen
    "Resize the receiver to the full screen size."

    self resize
```

✔ "class FixedWindow instance method"
```
resizeToMaxScreen
    "Do not resize the receiver as it is a fixed size."

    self resizeNotAllowed
```

Sending the message **#resizeToMaxScreen** to either window class will result in the receiving window sending the appropriate message for resizing itself.

Guideline 122
Avoid **#class, #isKindOf:,** and **#isMemberOf:** to check for class membership.

Multiple Polymorphism

Multiple polymorphic expressions are those in which several elements of the expression may each be of a different type. In contrast, in a simple polymorphic expression, the receiver of a message may dynamically vary in type. In the simple case, the result of sending a message varies depending on receiver's type. In the multiple case, however, the code tends to use type testing and results in the procedural style of case analysis.

The double dispatching technique described in [**Ingalls** 86] helps eliminate this kind of case analysis. Using this technique, new objects can be added to the system without having to change the existing code.

Guideline 123
Simplify multiple polymorphic expressions by using double dispatching.

Suppose you have several graphical objects to be displayed on different display devices: a screen, a printer, or a clipboard.

In this case, a programmer might be tempted to write the following case statements:

Tips, Tricks, and Traps

✗   "Class Rectangle instance method"
`displayOn: aPort`
      "Display the receiver on the Port specified by aPort."

```
(aPort isMemberOf: Screen)
    ifTrue: ["code for displaying on screen"].
(aPort isMemberOf: Printer)
    ifTrue: ["code for displaying on printer"].
(aPort isMemberOf: ClipBoard)
    ifTrue: ["code for displaying on clip board"]
```

The solution to these polymorphic messages is to use a relay method in each object to be displayed, as follows:

✔   "Class Rectangle instance method"
`displayOn: aPort`
      "Display the receiver on the Port specified by aPort."

```
aPort displayRectangle: self
```

"Class Circle instance method"
`displayOn: aPort`
      "Display the receiver on the Port specified by aPort."

```
aPort displayCircle: self
```

"Class Line instance method"
`displayOn: aPort`
      "Display the receiver on the Port specified by aPort."

```
aPort displayLine: self
```

To complete the dispatching, define the following for the display Port classes:

✔   "Class Screen instance methods"
`displayRectangle: aRectangle`
      "Display aRectangle on the receiver."

      "...code to display a rectangle on a screen..."

`displayCircle: aCircle`
      "Display aCircle on the receiver."

      "...code to display a circle on a screen..."

`displayLine: aLine`
      "Display aLine on the receiver."

      "...code to display a line on a screen..."

Similarly, define methods for the other objects to be displayed:

✔ "Class Printer instance methods"
displayRectangle: aRectangle
   "Display aRectangle on the receiver."

   "...code to display a rectangle on a printer..."

displayCircle: aCircle
   "Display aCircle on the receiver."

   "...code to display a circle on a printer..."

displayLine: aLine
   "Display aLine on the receiver."

   "...code to display a line on a printer..."

Reduce Case Analysis by using Table Lookup

Case analysis is often used to check a variable for possible values or to perform some action depending on the value. The use of a *Dictionary* can assist in eliminating this type of case statement.

☞ **Guideline 124**
Use table lookup to reduce the complexity of control structures.

Example
"Nested conditions - convert English accented vowels to German."

✘
```
englishPhoneme = 'oe'
    ifTrue: [
        germanPhoneme := 'ö']
    ifFalse: [
        englishPhoneme = 'ue'
            ifTrue: [
                germanPhoneme := 'ü']
            ifFalse: [
                englishPhoneme = 'ae'
                    ifTrue: [
                        germanPhoneme := 'ä']
                    ifFalse: [
                        germanPhoneme := englishPhoneme]]].
^germanPhoneme
```

✔ "Using a Dictionary"

```
phonemeMapping := Dictionary new.
phonemeMapping
    at: 'ae' put: 'ä';
    at: 'oe' put: 'ö';
    at: 'ue' put: 'ü'.


germanPhoneme := phonemeMapping
    at: englishPhoneme
    ifAbsent: [englishPhoneme].
```

The second argument to **#at:ifAbsent:** provides the same function as the default clause of a case statement.

Reorganize Deeply Nested Control Structures

Deeply nested control structures are difficult to comprehend and maintain.

Example

✗ "The following is part of a method that checks to see which key has been pressed."

```
normalKeyRange := 8r200.
(keyPressed < normalKeyRange)
    ifTrue: [self normalKeyAt: keyPressed put: value]
    ifFalse: [
        (keyPressed = CtrlKey)
            ifTrue: [ctrlState := value bitShift: 1]
            ifFalse: [
                (keyPressed = LeftShiftKey)
                    ifTrue: [leftShiftState := value]
                    ifFalse: [
                        (keyPressed = RightShiftKey)
                            ifTrue: [
                                rightShiftState := value]
                            ifFalse: [
                                (keyPressed = LockKey)
                                    ifTrue: [...]]]].
    metaState := ctrlState bitOr:
        (leftShiftState bitOr: rightShiftState)]
```

Divide up a single large method into separate submethods. This replaces the nested conditions with methods for each major condition. Each of these methods returns to the caller whenever the appropriate key has been processed.

✔ "The following is part of a method that checks which key has been pressed."

```
normalKeyRange := 8r200.
(keyPressed < normalKeyRange )
    ifTrue: [self normalKeyAt: keyPressed put: value]
    ifFalse: [
        self specialKeyAt: keyPressed put: value.
        metaState := ctrlState bitOr:
            (leftShiftState bitOr: rightShiftState)].
```

"Add this method to the class in which **#normalKeyAt:put:** is defined."

```
specialKeyAt: keyPressed put: aValue
    "Set the appropriate state of the receiver according to the
    keyPressed. Answer the receiver."

    (keyPressed = CtrlKey)
        ifTrue: [
            ctrlState := value bitShift: 1.
            ^self].
    (keyPressed = LeftShiftKey)
        ifTrue: [
            leftShiftState := value.
            ^self].
    (keyPressed = RightShiftKey)
        ifTrue: [
            rightShiftState := value.
            ^self].
```

Avoid the Use of Systems Programming Methods

There are a number of methods in Object and Behavior that should be used only when absolutely required: **#become:**, **#isKindOf:**, **#isMemberOf:**, **#class**, **#instVar:**, **#perform**, **#update**, **#doesNotUnderstand**. These methods all have important uses in the Smalltalk development environment where they are required, but they are usually unnecessary in application code. See Guideline 122 on page 98 for related information.

Abuse of Blocks

Blocks are a powerful programming construct much like first-class lexical closures. Unfortunately, not all Smalltalk implementations create a lexical scope for each block so nested and recursive blocks should be avoided. The ability to create a block of code and execute it later under program control often attracts the novice to use blocks instead of defining explicit methods. The use of large numbers of blocks makes code very difficult to debug since the blocks themselves are anonymous.

☞ **Guideline 125**
Avoid nested and recursive blocks when explicit methods are more appropriate.

Example

Replace the blocks with explicit messages for each.

 "Perform an action depending on the relationship between x and y."
```
someMethod
    action1 := [...code1].
    action2 := [...code2].
    (x < y)
        ifTrue: [action1 value]
        ifFalse: [action2 value].
```

✔ "Perform an action depending on the relationship between x and y."
```
action1
    "method"
    code1

action2
    "method"
    code2

someMethod
    (x < y)
        ifTrue: [self action1]
        ifFalse: [self action2].
```

Collection Operations Versus Counter-Controlled Loops

Smalltalk provides blocks to allow the programmer to use higher-level control structures. Using these makes the code easier to read than counter-controlled for-loops. The collection methods **#do:**, **#collect:**, **#select:**, **#reject:**, **#inject:** should be used instead of **#to:do:** whenever possible.

 Guideline 126

Use **#do:**, **#collect:**, **#select:**, **#reject:**, **#inject:** instead of **#to:do:** whenever possible.

Example
✗ `1 to: aCollection size do: [:index | ... ].`
✔ `aCollection do: [:element | ... ].`

✗
```
| result |
result := OrderedCollection new.
1 to: aCollection size do: [:index |
    result add: (aCollection at: index) name].
```

✔ `aCollection collect: [:element | element name].`

Potential Sources of Abuse and Misuse   103

Summary of Guidelines

The guidelines in this section have been shortened so they can act as a quick reference for the reader. To see the complete guideline with its explanation and examples, see the appropriate page indicated.

Summary of Guidelines

GLOSSARY

abstract class

A class that specifies a common protocol that is to be implemented differently by subclasses. The abstract class does not provide a full implementation. Its subclasses may have different representations. Abstract classes are not instantiated.

abstraction

A view of a problem that extracts the essential information relevant to a particular purpose and ignores the remainder of the information.

basic Smalltalk

Off-the-shelf Smalltalk with no extra tools or goodies.

binary message

A message with one argument and a selector that is one of a set of special single or double characters. For example +, /, -, ==, //, and ~=.

block

A literal method; an object representing a sequence of actions to be taken at a later time, upon receiving an "evaluation" message, such as with the selector value or value:. In Smalltalk, blocks are denoted by []. A block is similar to the LISP lambda expression.

class instance variable

A variable shared by all instances of a given class and the class itself.

cascaded message

A cascaded message is a shorthand way of writing a series of messages that are sent to the same receiver. For example,

```
Dog new
    bark;
    playDead;
    run: 100;
    home.
```

class variable

A variable shared by a class, its subclasses, and all instances of the class and its subclasses.

class

A description of one or more similar objects. A class is the program module of an object-oriented program because it describes a data structure called an object, algorithms called methods, and external interfaces called message protocol. In Smalltalk, every object is an instance of some class.

collaborations

The requests from a client class to a server class to fulfill a client responsibility. An object collaborates with another if it sends the other object any messages to fulfill a responsibility.

component

A grouping of classes that together perform some useful function such as a special menu system or an editor.

consumer class

A class that uses (consumes) another class to perform a specific task.

constructor class

A class used for building complex objects in a user-friendly notation or special-purpose language.

contravariance

A description of the parameter relationship in the context of type substitution. The corresponding parameter relationship is opposite to the relationship of the two types being compared.

covariance

A description of the return value relationship in the context of type substitution. The corresponding return values parallel the relationship of the two types being compared.

data abstraction

The result of extracting and retaining only the essential characteristic properties of data by defining specific data types and their associated functional characteristics, thus separating and hiding the representation details.

dynamic binding

The notion that the operation indicated is determined at run-time rather than compile-time. This permits operations to be overloaded for very large numbers of classes; for example, operations like =, inspect, and copy. It also permits libraries that were created and compiled long ago to apply to new classes of objects that did not exist when the libraries were created.

encapsulation

The technique of isolating a system function within a module and providing a precise specification for the module.

enumeration

The ability to sequence through a collection element by element.

extension

The addition of a new feature or function that is a pure augmentation of the system. A change is an extension if and only if it does not change the normal behavior of the underlying system that is being extended [**Jacobson** 95].

file-in

An ASCII file composed of Smalltalk source code that can be exchanged with other images. The process of reading in Smalltalk code from an external file.

framework

A set of abstract classes with a common protocol that permit the user to easily reuse libraries of code.

get method

A method that "gets" or retrieves the value of a state variable.

global variable

A variable shared by all of the classes and their instances.

hierarchy

A structure whose components are ranked into levels of subordination according to a specific set of rules.

information hiding

The technique of encapsulating software design decisions in a module in such a way that the module's interface reveals as little as possible about the module's inner workings; thus, each module is a "black box" to the other modules in the system. The discipline of information hiding forbids the use of information about a module that is not in the module's interface specification.

instance

An object described by a particular class.

instance variable

A variable which expresses a state or attribute of an object.

"is-a" relationship

A specialization relationship. It describes one kind of object as a special case of another.

keyword message

A message that has one or more arguments and a selector made up of a series of identifiers with trailing colons, one preceding each argument. For example,

    aPoint translateBy: aVector.

literal object

An object that can be described literally in Smalltalk, including Numbers, Strings, Characters, Symbols, and Arrays. For example,

    54213
    'magic'
    $c
    #red
    #(1 2 4 red green blue)

long keyword message

A message composed of multiple parameters. For example,

    menu
        add: selector
        label: label
        enable: enable

message

A method applied to an object. A request sent to an object to perform some task.

metaclass

A class whose single instance is itself a class.

method

A procedure-like entity; the description of a sequence of actions to be taken when a message is received by an object. A routine.

method dictionary

A set of associations between message selectors and methods included in each class description.

multiple polymorphic expression

An expression in which several elements may each be of a different type.

name space

The collection of names that have been assigned to Smalltalk classes.

nil

A special object that is an instance of class *UndefinedObject*; it is assigned to the instance variables of all new objects. This means that unless an object assigns a value to its instance variables, they contain nil.

object

A package of information and a description of its manipulation. More specifically, a package of information consists of a data structure and the manipulation of the data structure is accomplished by using subprograms called methods.

object management system

An object-oriented database that is used for storing and retrieving objects.

overloading

The notion that objects of many different types can have operations with the same name without ambiguity, operations such as = , display, or print. It is essential for polymorphism and extendibility.

parameter

One of the objects specified in a message that provides information needed so that a message receiver can be manipulated appropriately.

persistent object

An object that outlives the program that created it. An object that is to be shared between different programs such as a dictionary of icons in a disk file.

polymorphism

A unique characteristic of object-oriented programming whereby different objects respond to the same message with their own unique behavior. For example, many different objects respond to the **#display** message.

pool dictionary

A set of associations shared by instances of several classes.

primitives

System- or user-defined subroutines accessed by Smalltalk to perform some *primitive* or time-critical operation such as addition. User-defined primitives offer a way of interfacing non-Smalltalk based code such as assembly, C, or FORTRAN into a Smalltalk program.

private method

A method not intended for general public code development which is used to support the function of another method. A private method is not guaranteed to maintain the same functions or even exist in future revisions of the code. The private nature of a method is explicitly noted in the method's comments.

protocol

A set of standard messages that a collection of classes is expected to respond to.

pseudo-variable

A variable available in every method without special declaration, but whose value cannot be changed using an assignment. For example self and super.

public method

A stable method sanctioned for general use by other code developers. By making a method public, the author of the method assumes the commitment to not alter the intended functions of the public method through future code revisions.

receiver

The object to be manipulated, according to a message.

refactoring

Identifying a common attribute, such as shared behavior in classes, and redesigning the class hierarchy such that the behavior is captured in one place. Subclasses would inherit this behavior, typically from an abstract class.

reusability

The extent to which a module can be reused.

robustness

The extent to which software can continue to operate correctly despite the introduction of invalid inputs.

selector

A part of a message that specifies the operation requested.

self

The pseudo-variable that refers to the receiver of a message.

sender

The object requesting a manipulation.

set method

A method that "sets" or assigns the value of a state variable.

state variables

The variables representing the state of an object. This term is used when referring to the instance variables, class variables, and class instance variables of a class.

subclass

A class that is created by sharing the description of another class, often modifying some aspects of that description.

subclassing

Also called inheritance. An implementation mechanism for sharing code and representation.

subtyping

A substitution relationship. An instance of a subtype can stand in for an instance of its supertype.

temporary variable

A variable that exists only while the method in which it is declared is in the process of execution.

unary message

A message without arguments. For example, factorial in 10 **factorial**.

REFERENCES

[ACM 94] *Object-Oriented Software Testing*. Communications of the ACM 37(9). ACM Press. September 1994.

[Baecker 90] Baecker, R. and Marcus. *Human Factors and Typography for More Readable Programs*. Addison-Wesley. Massachusetts. 1990.

[Barry 89] Barry, B. Prototyping a Real-Time Embedded System in Smalltalk. *Proceedings of OOPSLA '89*, New Orleans. ACM SIGPLAN. 1989.

[Beck 94] Beck, K. Simple Smalltalk testing. pp 16-18, *The Smalltalk Report 4(2)*. October 1994.

[Bentley 86] Bentley, J. Programming Pearls: Little Languages. pp.711-721, *Communcations of the ACM 29(8)*. August 1986.

[Berard 92] Berard, E. *Testing Object-Oriented Software*, Tutorial No. 30 Notes, OOPSLA '92 Conference. Vancouver, BC. 1992.

[Budd 87] Budd, T. *A Little Smalltalk*. Addison-Wesley. 1987.

[Coad 89] Coad, P. and Yourdon, E. *Object Oriented Analysis*. Prentice Hall. 1990.

[Goldberg 83] Goldberg, A. and Robson, D. *Smalltalk-80: The language and Its Implementation*. Addison-Wesley. Reading. MA. 1983.

[Goldberg 84] Goldberg, A. *Smalltalk-80: The Interactive Programming Environment*. Addison-Wesley. Reading. MA. 1984.

[Halstead 77] Halstead, M.H., *Elements of Software Science*, pp. 274-279, Elsiver, New York. 1977.

[Ingalls 86] Ingalls, D. A Simple Technique for Handling Multiple Polymorphism. pp. 347-349, *Proceedings of OOPSLA '86*, Portland, Or., ACM SIGPLAN 21(11). 1986.

[Jacobson 92] Jacobson, I., Christersson M., Jonsson P. and Overgaard G. *Object-Oriented Software Engineering - a Use Case Driven Approach*. Addison-Wesley. Reading. MA. 1992.

[Jacobson 95] Jacobson, I. and Thomas, D. Extensions - A Technique for Evolving Large Systems. Submitted for publication to ROAD. SIGS 1995.

[Johnson 88] Johnson, R. and Foote, B. Designing Reusable Classes. pp. 22-35, *Journal of Object-Oriented Programming*, June/July 1988.

[Johnson 93] Johnson, R. Classic Smalltalk Bugs. pp. 5-9, *The Smalltalk Report 2(7)*. May 1993.

[Kernighan 78] Kernighan, B.W. and Plauger, P.J. *The Elements of Programming Style*. McGraw-Hill, New York, 1978.

[LaLonde 88] LaLonde, W. and Pugh, J. Disk Forms, pp. 54-56, *Journal of Object Oriented Programming 1(4)*, November/December 1988.

[LaLonde 89] LaLonde, W. and Pugh, J. Finite State Machines (Automata) and Constructor Classes. pp. 56-62, *Journal of Object-Oriented Programming 2(4)*, November/December 1989.

[LaLonde 90A] LaLonde, W. and Pugh, J. *Inside Smalltalk Vol. 1*. Prentice Hall. 1990.

[LaLonde 90B] LaLonde, W. and Pugh, J. *Inside Smalltalk Vol. II*. Prentice Hall. 1990.

[LaLonde 91] LaLonde, W. and Pugh, J. Subclassing ~= subtyping ~= Is-a. pp. 57-62, *Journal of Object-Oriented Programming 3(5)*. January 1991.

[LaLonde 94A] LaLonde, W. *Discovering Smalltalk*. Benjamin Cummings, Redwood City, CA, 1994.

[LaLonde 94B] LaLonde, W. and Pugh, J. *Smalltalk V Practice and Experience*. Prentice Hall. 1994.

[Ledgard 79] Ledgard, H.F., Nagin, P.A. and Hueras, J.F. *Pascal with Style: Programming Proverbs*. Hayden Book Company, New Jersey. 1979.

[Ledgard 87] Ledgard, H. and Tauer, J. *Professional Software: Programming Practice*. Addison-Wesley, Massachusetts. 1987.

[Lieberherr 89] Lieberherr, K. and Holland, I. Assuring Good Style for Object-Oriented Programs. pp. 38-48, *IEEE Software*. September. 1989.

[Meyer 88] Meyer, B. Bidding Farewell to Globals. *Journal of Object-Oriented Programming*. August/September 1988.

[Perry 90] Perry, D.E. and Kaiser, G.E. Adequate Testing and Object-Oriented Programming. *Journal of Object-Oriented Programming*, January/February 1990.

[Rochat 86] Rochat, R. *In Search of Good Smalltalk Programming Style*. Technical Report CR-86-19, Tektronix, 1986.

[Rettig 91] Rettig, M. Testing Made Palatable, pp. 25-29, *Communications of the ACM, 34(5)*. 1991.

[Sandberg 88] Sandberg, D.W. Smalltalk and Exploratory Programming. pp. 85-92, *ACM SIGPLAN Notices 23(10)*. 1988.

[Shafer 93] Shafer, D., Herndon, S. and Rozier, L. *Smalltalk Programing for Windows*, Prima Publishing, Rocklin. Ca., 1993.

[Smith 94] Smith, D.N. *IBM Smalltalk: The Language*. Benjamin/Cummings Publishing, Redwood City, Ca. 1994.

[Snyder 86] Snyder, A. Encapsulation and Inheritance in Object-Oriented Programming Languages. pp 38-45, *Proceedings of OOPSLA '86*. ACM SIGPLAN. 1986.

[Soft 88] Software Productivity Consortium. *ADA Style Guide*. SPC-TR-88-003, 1988.

[Thomson 93] Thomson, D.G. *Believable Specifications: Organizing and Describing Object Interfaces Using Protocol Conformance*. Carleton University, Ottawa, Canada. School of Computer Science Master's Thesis, 1993.

[Siepmann 94] Siepmann, E. and Newton, A.R. TOBAC: A Test Case Browser for Testing of Object-Oriented Software. *Proceedings of International Symposium on Software Testing and Analysis (ISSTA)*. ACM 1994.

[Wirfs-Brock 89] Wirfs-Brock, A. and Wilkerson, B. Variables Limit Reusability. pp. 34-40, *Journal of Object-Oriented Programming*, May/June 1989.

[Wirfs-Brock 90] Wirfs-Brock, R., Wilkerson, B. and Wiener, L. *Designing Object-Oriented Software*. Prentice-Hall, 1990.

[Wulf 73] Wulf, W. and Shaw, M. Global Variable Considered Harmful. *ACM SIGPLAN Notices 8*, 1973.

INDEX

The Guidelines are indexed with page numbers in italic.

Definitions of terms are indexed with page numbers in bold.

Index